Studies in the Structure of the Urban Economy

Foreword

A decade ago the most informed analysis of land use and of the location of economic activities in the American city was to be found in a few books on urban real estate and land economics bearing such names as Homer Hoyt, Arthur Weimer, and Richard Ratcliffe. They were addressed to professionals in the real estate industry with an occasional translation for the benefit of city planners. They were wise and insightful but limited by their devotion to the needs of real estate practitioners, by their fundamentally institutional approach to the issues, and by their inability to deal analytically with the enormous number of behavioral variables that are involved in the social and economic processes that generate urban spatial organization. From this intellectual base evolved a flow of research on the space economy of the American city, which has not only improved our knowledge of how cities are organized but also equipped planners with more sophisticated mechanisms for thinking about alternative urban futures.

A decade ago, also, Resources for the Future published the study *Transportation and Urban Land*, the first step in a line of staff and sponsored research of which this book is the most recent product. In the course of the past ten years, the RFF Program in Urban Economics identified the economics of intra-urban organization as one of four major substantive fields to receive financial support and encouragement; grants and fellowships were awarded and scholarly conferences and seminars sponsored in an effort to accelerate the growth of knowledge and understanding about the processes that organize the use of space in American cities.

Simultaneously, a more general policy interest arose from the application of quantitative models to transportation planning in metropolitan areas, especially in their usefulness in highlighting the impact of changing transportation conditions on land use and the location of economic activity. Philadelphia's Penn-Jersey Transportation Study in the early 1960s pioneered the use of computer-based, large-scale models in planning transportation and land use in metropolitan areas, and from this experience—and the money and interest of the Bureau of Public Roads—a number of species of such models have been developed and used by urban planners and transportation experts.

The economics of the location of activities within the city has continued to intrigue a small but growing number of economists. Household location, the distribution of retail establishments, and the siting of industry have been the subjects of many dissertations written in the last decade, not a few of which were supported by RFF under its Urban Economics Doctoral Dissertation Fellowship Program.

At the end of the decade the state of knowledge consisted of several large-scale, comprehensive, applied, quantitative models whose eclectic characteristics should not detract from recognition of their ingenuity—they were developed for the purpose of making conditional predictions about the outcomes of the interaction between transportation systems and land use—and a variety of partial models produced by scholars incorporating economic propositions about behavior and welfare in their structures.

This book, the research behind which was supported by RFF, is the logical next step in the evolution of our understanding of the internal organization of cities. It develops a purely economic model to "explain" comprehensively, if at a large grain, the way in which cities are organized and how they tend to change, demonstrating the extent to which economic logic, which underlies the behavior of the multitude of markets in the city, is sufficient to account for major characteristics of urban growth and change. While it is not the conclusion of this line of work, it marks the successful outcome of a decade of research and analysis seeking to provide a more precise and thoroughgoing understanding of the nature of the urban space economy.

While the author's professional peers will appreciate the elegance of his mathematical analyses and the conciseness of his discussion of an extraordinarily complex set of problems, less expert readers also will learn much from his exposition. While what follows may not be the last word on quantitative economic models of the city, the last word—when it is uttered—will not be unfamiliar to any reader who has mastered the propositions formulated and tested by Professor Mills in this book.

Lowdon Wingo, *Director*
Regional and Urban Studies
August 1971   Resources for the Future

Preface

This monograph reports the results of several closely related research projects on the determinants of urban structure. The focus of the work is decentralization of metropolitan areas, which I believe to be one of the most intriguing issues in urban economics, as well as the key to many of the social problems found in urban areas.

The research reported here has been generously supported by Resources for the Future. I am deeply indebted to them and to Harvey Perloff and Lowdon Wingo for sympathy, understanding, and professional guidance. Irving Hoch undertook a perceptive and critical review of the entire manuscript. Helpful suggestions were also made by Britton Harris, John Meyer, and George Tolley. Computations and other assistance were performed by Richard Dillman, Tatsuo Hatta, Allen Spirer, and Mary Teplin.

For more than twenty years, I have generously shared the torments of scholarship with my wife, to whom this volume should be dedicated.

EDWIN S. MILLS

Princeton University

June 1971

Contents

List of Tables

Studies in the Structure of the
Urban Economy

Introduction

Urban economics is a neophyte among specialties in economics. There is therefore a relatively wide range of views concerning the questions that should be asked, the tools appropriate for analysis, and the assumptions that will best approximate the phenomena under study. Most urban specialists would probably agree that the purpose of urban areas, broadly interpreted, is to facilitate production and exchange by proximate locations of producers and consumers. In this view, a city that grows as a seat of government is to be explained by the advantages of proximity to agencies producing public services and by the advantages to related private activities of locating close to the seat of government. Likewise, a great industrial city grows around a port because it is profitable to produce at a place where interregional or international trade is cheap. The extent and spatial form of the resulting concentration of activity depend on a host of economic, institutional, technological, and geographical considerations.

In the United States and in most other western societies, land is allocated among alternative uses mainly in private markets, with more or less public regulation. In such societies, urban areas result mainly from locational decisions by large numbers of private producers and consumers, each attempting to further the self-interest of the decision-making group. The purpose of this monograph is to present a set of closely related studies of the ways that private markets determine urban structure in an economic setting such as that in the United States. Specifically, most of the studies focus on one aspect or another of the decentralization of urban areas that has been in progress for many decades.

Urban economics, like other specialties in economics, has both positive and normative aspects. Some of the most difficult and fundamental issues in urban economics have to do with the circumstances under which markets are an efficient means of resource allocation. The main focus of the monograph is positive economics. It is intended as a contribution to the understanding of market operations in an urban context. Nevertheless, there is theoretical analysis of market efficiency in two of the models that

1

follow. There is also discussion of ways that the models could be modified and extended so that they could be used to evaluate public policies. But there is no substantial evaluation of any urban public policies in the chapters that follow.

The book may be outlined as follows:

Chapter 1 is preliminary in nature. It develops the rationale of an urban area that was alluded to above and that underlies the rest of the book.

Chapter 2 places the subsequent analysis in historical perspective. It surveys the broad outlines of urban growth and structure in the United States.

Chapter 3 is a detailed empirical study of a special aspect of urban structure. It is concerned with the pattern of land use intensity for residential and employment purposes. Population and employment density functions are estimated and studied for a sample of United States metropolitan areas between 1880 and 1963.

Chapter 4 is a transition between the early empirically oriented chapters and the subsequent theoretically oriented chapters. It surveys a sample of prominent models of urban growth and structure that were formulated during the 1960s.

Chapter 5 presents one of the simplest theoretical models of urban structure that can be formulated. Its simplicity permits a complete analysis of both positive and normative aspects of market performance.

Chapter 6 introduces the book's major theoretical model of urban structure. A moderately large simultaneous equation model is formulated to study the relationships between residential location and commuting. The chapter contains preliminary analysis of the model's properties and indicates how important properties can be ascertained using numerical analysis on a computer.

Chapter 7 presents an elaborate numerical analysis of the model introduced in chapter 6. It studies the effects of changes in all the model's parameters on the pattern of urban residential location.

Chapter 8 presents and analyzes a model that is closely related to the one analyzed in the two preceding chapters. It differs from the earlier model in that the realistic and congested transportation system in the earlier model is replaced by an idealized system that obeys the conditions of economic efficiency. Comparison between the models suggests the effects that a policy of efficient investment and pricing in urban transportation might have on the pattern of urban residential density.

Chapter 9 concludes the book with some suggestions for ways in which the models could be extended for public policy analysis and with suggestions for further research.

1

Some Qualitative Considerations

The following chapters analyze several models pertaining to the structure and functions of urban areas. Some assumptions are peculiar to particular models and they are stated at appropriate places in the book. But there is a general view of the nature of urban areas that underlies all the research reported here. The purpose of this chapter is to set out that view as carefully as possible. The ideas put forth are not particularly original. Many are scattered more or less explicitly through the work of urban economists and geographers, most notably the classic work of August Lösch [15]. The intent here is to present the ideas in a concise and coherent framework, using terminology familiar to economists.

Generically, a city is a place where population density is high compared to that of the surrounding area. Since people normally live in houses, it is almost an equivalent to say that a city is a place where the ratios of other inputs, especially capital, to land are high in the production of housing services compared to those of the surrounding area. People normally work close to their places of residence, and cities are therefore also characterized by high densities of employment and production of other goods and services. Thus, quite generally, a city can be characterized as a place where land is used intensively, i.e., where ratios of outputs and other inputs to land are higher than in the surrounding area.

One way that intensive land use is achieved in urban areas is by the exclusion of activities, such as agriculture, whose production functions are not appropriately land-intensive. Indeed, since agriculture has the lowest output-land ratio of broadly defined industries, a definition of a city that used an output-land ratio only slightly higher than that in surrounding areas would imply that all nonagricultural land was urban. But most data sources employ definitions of urban areas that make it possible for many productive activities to take place outside urban areas. Some data on this matter will be presented in chapter 2.

The second way that intensive land use is achieved in urban areas is by employing more nonland inputs per unit of output of particular goods and services there than elsewhere. Many goods and services are produced in both urban and rural areas, but they are produced with different factor proportions in the two places.

1. A WORLD WITHOUT CITIES

It is useful to start with some assumptions that have been widely used in general equilibrium theory, but that imply that there would be no cities. Consider a general equilibrium model in which there is a finite number of intermediate and final goods. There are, however, only two homogeneous nonproduced factors of production: land and labor. All inputs and outputs are perfectly divisible. Among the intermediate goods are transportation services, used for both freight and commuters. All production and utility functions have the usual neoclassical properties, and there are constant returns to scale in each industry. All input and output markets are perfectly competitive.

Workers' utility functions contain only the amounts of produced goods and services they consume, and the inputs they supply. Workers choose their places of residence so as to maximize utility—i.e., they are perfectly mobile; land is by definition perfectly immobile, but it is available in uniform quantity everywhere.

In the world just described, land rents would be the same everywhere and each acre of land would contain the same number of people and the same mix of productive activities. The crucial point in establishing this result is that constant returns permit each productive activity to be carried on at an arbitrarily low level without loss of efficiency. Furthermore, all land is equally productive and equilibrium requires that the value of its marginal product, and hence its rent, be the same everywhere. Therefore, in equilibrium, all the inputs and outputs necessary directly and indirectly to meet the demands of consumers can be located in a small area near where consumers live. In that way, each small area can be autarkic and transportation of people and goods can be avoided. Any attempt to change the allocation so as to produce a nonuniform distribution of production and people would raise land values wherever there was a concentration of activity. Workers living in the concentrated area could then increase their consumption of goods and services by moving to a low-density area. Furthermore, if production differed from consumption in any area, scarce resources would have to be devoted to transportation. If each small area is autarkic, these resources can instead be devoted to the production of final consumption goods and services.

The crucial assumptions in this model are constant returns to scale and a uniform distribution of land. It is practically impossible to produce concentration or agglomeration of economic activity in a model with these characteristics. Some scholars write as though the desire to avoid transportation costs were sufficient to produce agglomeration. They assume that workers congregate around places of work to avoid commuting costs and costs of shipping goods from places of production to places of residence. But the result depends crucially on the existence of scale economies. In the absence of scale economies, the desire to avoid transportation costs leads to the opposite result, namely a uniform density of population and economic activity.

2. Reasons for Cities

There are of course many ways of altering the assumptions in the previous section so as to account for the existence of cities. The procedure in this section will be to introduce the major changes that seem to me to be important in understanding agglomeration.

The simplest change in the model that would account for agglomeration is to recognize differences among countries. Suppose that all the assumptions in section 1 continue to hold within each country. But suppose that countries differ from each other as to the properties of production functions, tastes of consumers, or endowments of nonproduced factors of production. Suppose further that these differences make trade among countries desirable. Then each country can economize on transportation of traded goods by concentrating economic activity near the borders that are closest to its trading partners. It will be advantageous to locate near the borders for both producers of exports and consumers of imports. Then producers of inputs used in the export industry will also tend to locate near the borders, and so will domestic producers of consumer goods to be sold to residents there. Following the argument further, we can say that producers and consumers directly and indirectly related to international trade will locate near the borders in such a way that land values there will be enough higher than land values elsewhere to justify locating elsewhere and incurring extra transportation costs. The result will be a land rent function and density of population and economic activity that fall with distance from the borders. Undoubtedly, international trade has been historically important in causing the concentration of United States population and economic activity along the Atlantic, Pacific, and Gulf coasts and along the Great Lakes.

The next step is to recognize that the factors that account for trade among countries can also account for trade among regions of a country.

Just as production functions, tastes, and nonproduced factor endowments may vary among countries, so they may also vary from place to place within a country. But technology, tastes, and human resources vary relatively little within a country since movement and communication are much easier within than between countries. Thus, the major source of comparative advantage among regions within a country is variability in the amounts of nonproduced material resources. Specifically, contrary to the assumption in section 1, land is not a single uniformly distributed resource. Rather, many kinds of natural resources, such as minerals, land forms, and climate are used in production, and their availability differs greatly from one place to another within a country.

Regional variation in natural resource availability provides a justification for regional specialization in production and for two-way, interregional trade. It follows that population and economic activity will to some extent be concentrated within and among regions. But regional variation in natural resource availability affects not only the production of goods but also the production of interregional transportation. Therefore, regional agglomerations of population and economic activity tend to be located at places where interregional trade is especially cheap. Navigable waterways are the best examples, but land well suited for road and rail transportation and for air terminals produces the same effect. Of course, to some extent the natural conditions that make an area desirable as a center for interregional trade and for the production and consumption of traded goods also make it desirable as a center for international trade.

In the discussion so far, the emphasis has been on regional and international differences in natural resource endowments as determinants of agglomeration. These differences are real and important, and they have been emphasized by geographers, regional scientists, and location theorists such as Weber [35]. But other location theorists, especially Lösch [15], have retained the assumption that natural resources are uniformly distributed and have instead dropped the assumption of constant returns to scale to account for agglomeration.

To pursue this idea, return to the assumptions made in section 1, but suppose there is one production function with increasing returns to scale. It is unfortunate that economists have devoted so little attention to the role of land as an input. Aside from those pertaining to agriculture, production function studies almost never include land among the inputs. Yet the land-intensity of various production processes and the substitutability between land and other inputs, especially structures, are major determinants of decentralization in urban areas. In particular, economists have said practically nothing about the relationship between contiguity and scale economies. In some examples, as in the case of materials that must be at very high or very low temperatures at several productive stages, spatial proximity of processes is clearly important. Presumably, a good generalization is that scale economies that are intraplant require proximity but those that are interplant do not. But on reasonable definitions, the generalization is tautological. A plant is presumably to be defined as a contiguous set of productive processes under a single control. What is needed is a specification of circumstances under which contiguity increases productivity.

For the sake of simplicity, assume that scale economies require contiguous production. Then equilibrium will require that the product subject to scale economies be produced in large amounts at some places and not at all elsewhere. Then suppliers of produced inputs, not subject to scale economies, will find it advantageous to produce at greater output-land ratios near the firm with scale economies than elsewhere, in order to economize on transportation costs. Likewise, workers in the firm with scale economies and consumers of its output will find it advantageous to locate near the plant and to live in houses that economize on land. Following the argument a second step, so will suppliers of suppliers and producers of other goods sold to consumers located near the firm with scale economies. In this way equilibrium will produce an agglomeration or urban area centered on production of the commodity with scale economies, and with land values, population density, and output-land ratios that fall with distance from the center of the urban area. The entire country would consist of a set of similar urban areas.

We thus see that scale economies can account for cities in much the way that regional comparative advantage can account for them. But there is a difference. Unlike the cities generated by regional comparative advantage, the cities generated by scale economies do not trade with each other. Each such city may trade with its surrounding hinterland, but not with other cities.

Now enrich the model by supposing that there is a second industry with scale economies. Lösch has shown that then, in some circumstances, some cities will contain both industries with scale economies and other cities will contain only one. Lösch was mainly interested in the case in which both industries make final-consumption goods. The circumstances in question depend on the extent of scale economies, demand for the products, and transportation costs. In this model, the city that produces both goods subject to scale economies would export one of the goods to other cities that do not produce both goods. But trade would be only one way.

Generalizing further, Lösch considered a model in which each industry was subject to scale economies that were exhausted at output levels which satisfied demands of different numbers of customers. With very restrictive assumptions, Lösch built an entire theory of a hierarchy of city sizes on this basis. The cities can now trade with each other in a special way. Each city of a certain size will export to cities of smaller size, but small cities can sell nothing to larger cities. In this respect, Lösch's ingenious model is rather rigid, but it leads to an important insight concerning cities.

Economists tend to think of scale economies mainly in connection with manufacturing industry, but in fact they are pervasive. Scale economies are important to the extent that the output level at which they are exhausted is large in relation to the firm's demand. There are many highly specialized business and consumer services for which demand per customer is very small. Good examples are found among legal, medical, and financial services. In many such activities, scale economies are exhausted only at demand levels so large that they can be generated only in large cities. It is for that reason that many specialized services are available only in cities exceeding certain sizes.

The concept of scale economies also provides important insights regarding the structure of urban areas. Some activities locate near city centers because they sell their products locally and scale economies are exhausted only at demand levels that require all the customers in the urban area. They locate near the city center because it provides maximum accessibility. A second set of activities, especially in manufacturing, exports large parts of its output. Although the manufacturers may need to produce on a large scale to exhaust scale economies, they have no need for central location for access to local customers. For them, central location is valuable mainly if it provides easy access to cheap means of intercity trade. But to the extent that the mode used for intercity trade is highways rather than water or rail, suburban locations provide better access than do central locations. A third set of activities sells mainly to local customers and has scale economies exhausted by the demand of only part of the urban area's population. These activities tend to locate in subcenters outside the city center. The suburban shopping center is the paradigm, but services are also increasingly provided in such subcenters. Subcenters are more important the larger the urban area, the greater the per capita demand, the smaller the output level at which scale economies are exhausted, and the greater the transportation costs. In particular, high downtown transportation costs resulting from congestion obviously spur the development of subcenters.

So far, regional comparative advantage and scale economies have been used to account for the existence of cities. A third factor that has been given increasing attention in recent years has been referred to as amenity resources.[1] Amenity resources are natural conditions that enter directly into people's utility functions. Just as regional differences in natural resource availability can account for regional comparative advantage in production, so regional differences in natural resources can account for regional comparative advantage in consumption. Some people have strong preferences for a variety of natural conditions such as sunshine, warmth, salt water beaches, or mountain slopes for skiing. It seems likely that amenity resources have been important in accounting for rapid post–World War II growth of cities in the Southwest and in Florida. It also seems likely that there is a high income elasticity of demand for amenity resources. Amenity resources may be available throughout a large region, in which case they affect the regional distribution of population and economic activity but do not account for cities. Alternatively, particularly attractive vectors of amenities may be available in such a small area that the entire area becomes urbanized. The Los Angeles basin is such an area.

The argument in this chapter can be summarized as follows. There are two sets of characteristics that account for the existence of cities. One is scale economies in production of goods and services. The other is regional differences in natural conditions that affect production, people's utilities, and the cost of interregional trade.

Within this framework, the function of cities is to facilitate production and exchange by proximate locations of a variety of economic activities. The basic reason for proximity may be the existence of one or more industries with scale economies or the existence of regional comparative advantage in production and of points from which interregional trade is especially cheap. Proximity comes about partly by the exclusion of industries that require large amounts of land and partly by the use of higher ratios of other inputs to land in the city than elsewhere. The advantage of proximity is low transportation and exchange costs. The disadvantage is diminishing returns to the ratios of nonland inputs to land inputs. City sizes are determined by public and private decisions regarding the trade-off between the two sets of considerations.

1. See Perloff and others [30].

2

Trends in United States Urban
Growth and Structure

The purpose of this chapter is to survey historical trends in the growth
and structure of urban areas in the United States. Although some of the
trends discussed below have not been emphasized by other writers, little
of the material is new. The reasons for including the chapter are to bring
together and summarize results that seem interesting and relevant, and
to provide motivation for the analysis in subsequent chapters.

Several urban concepts are employed in this chapter, depending
mainly on data availability but also on the focus of enquiry. Some data for
legal cities and, more generally, urban places are available back to the
first census in 1790. But only since World War II have we had comprehensive data on metropolitan areas, and for that reason most of the data
presented in this chapter pertain to the period since 1945. The major postwar innovation has been the publication of data for Standard Metropolitan Statistical Areas (SMSAs) and of data for the economically more
meaningful urbanized areas, unfortunately much less complete. Using
census data for cities and counties, it is possible to construct data for
metropolitan areas for census years before World War II. The next chapter
analyzes data constructed in this way, going back to the nineteenth century, for a small sample of metropolitan areas. But a great deal of preliminary and somewhat subjective processing of data is necessary to
construct metropolitan area data for those years. Therefore, only limited
sampling is feasible.

The data analyzed in this chapter have of course been processed in
various ways that are described in the following sections. Neither the
choice of data to survey nor the manipulations performed upon them are
independent of hypotheses concerning urban growth and structure. Much
of the analysis is intended to provide at least preliminary insight into the
hypotheses introduced in later chapters. Nevertheless the focus of the
present chapter is descriptive rather than explanatory.

Table 1. *Urban and Rural Population of Coterminous United States, 1790–1970*
(population figures in millions)

Year	Total population	Urban population		Rural population	
		Number	Percent	Number	Percent
1790	3.9	0.2	5.1	3.7	94.9
1800	5.3	0.3	6.1	5.0	93.9
1810	7.2	0.5	7.3	6.7	92.7
1820	9.6	0.7	7.2	8.9	92.8
1830	12.9	1.1	8.8	11.7	91.2
1840	17.1	1.8	10.8	15.2	89.2
1850	23.2	3.5	15.3	19.6	84.7
1860	31.4	6.2	19.8	25.2	80.2
1870	38.6	9.9	25.7	28.7	74.3
1880	50.2	14.1	28.2	36.0	71.8
1890	62.9	22.1	35.1	40.8	64.9
1900	76.0	30.2	39.7	45.8	60.3
1910	92.0	42.0	45.7	50.0	54.3
1920	105.7	54.2	51.2	51.6	48.8
1930	122.8	69.0	56.2	53.8	43.8
1940	131.7	74.4	56.5	57.2	43.5
1950	150.7	89.7	59.6	60.9	40.4
1960	178.5	112.5	63.1	65.9	36.9
1970[1]	203.2	149.3	73.5	53.9	26.5

Sources: U.S. Census of Population, 1960, 1970.
Note: Numbers may not add to totals because of rounding.
[1] Based on new urban definition. Not comparable with earlier data.

1. URBANIZATION OF THE POPULATION

It is of course a commonplace observation that the United States has been transformed from a rural to an urban society during the nearly 200 years of its existence. The basic census data on which the observation is based are presented in table 1.

Since there is no unique or widely accepted definition of an urban area, it is always important to know the urban concept on which data are based. The urban population data in table 1 refer to the number of people living in urban places, the most inclusive urban concept used by the census. An urban place is an area, usually incorporated as a city, town, or village, containing at least 2,500 people, and any surrounding thickly settled but unincorporated area.[1] Under a new and slightly less restrictive definition of urban places, for which data are available only since 1950, the urban population was about seven percentage points greater in 1960 than the figure in table 1. For 1970, only the new definition is available, and it appears in table 1. In 1960, the census identified 5,445 urban

1. Precise definitions of all urban area concepts are given in the front of each census volume.

places. Since there are only about 200 large metropolitan areas in the United States, the urban place is an extremely inclusive notion, encompassing large numbers of villages and small towns.

Table 1 shows that both the urban and the rural population increased during every decade from 1790 to 1960. The percentage of the population that is urban, however, has also increased during every decade (except for a trivial drop from 1810 to 1820), going from 5.1 percent in 1790 to 73.5 percent in 1970. This dramatic change has justifiably elicited extensive comment in popular writing. It is indeed one of the most significant characterizations of United States economic history. It is also noteworthy that the fastest growth in the percentage of the population that was urban took place during the nine decades between 1840 and 1930. During that period the percentage of the population that was urban increased by an average of 5 percentage points per decade. From 1790 to 1840, it increased by an average of 1.1 percentage points per decade. And from 1930 to 1960, it increased by an average of 1.7 percentage points per decade. Between 1940 and 1960 the percentage of the population that was urban has increased by between 3 and 4 percentage points per decade. If the old definition were available for 1970, it would probably show about the same trend. Some of the postwar urbanization clearly would have occurred during the 1930s had it not been for the depression. Despite this, the postwar rate, as measured here, is much less than the rate between 1840 and 1930.

These data confirm the widely held view that industrialization and urbanization are related. Urbanization proceeded relatively slowly before the time of the Civil War. Its pace quickened during the period of rapid industrialization in the last half of the nineteenth century and early part of the twentieth. What is not so widely appreciated is that, as industrialization has become widespread, and as the growth rate of employment in manufacturing has slackened, the rate of urbanization has declined.

It is also important to note that, even under the new and inclusive urban concept, the census still classified one-third of the population as rural in 1960 and one-fourth in 1970. Thus, it is by no means true that rural areas have been drained of population, either absolutely or proportionately. The deceleration of the urbanization process therefore results from a weakening of the forces that cause urban growth, and not merely from a lack of population in rural areas. Finally, it should be noted that the rural population is much larger than the farm population. The farm population fell from 32 million in 1920 to 15 million in 1960. During the same period, the rural population grew from 52 million to 66 million. Thus, a growing majority of rural residents are nonfarm. As will be pointed out in the next section, substantial percentages of employment are outside urban areas in many industries.

It is important not to infer too much from these figures. All that has been established is that the growth of the percentage of the population living in urban places accelerated during the period of rapid industrialization and decelerated after about 1930. We do not know how many rural residents worked in urban places. Some rural residents certainly live in SMSAs, since substantial parts of most SMSAs are rural. Furthermore, as will be shown in the next section, substantial amounts of manufacturing employment are in rural areas. There seems to be a prima facie case that the deceleration in urbanization is related to the stagnation of manufacturing employment, but the relationship is probably neither simple nor very strong. Under practically any theory of urbanization, the percentage of the population that was urban would grow more slowly as the percentage became large. But it is interesting to note that it has happened in the United States.[2]

For most purposes, the SMSA is a more useful urban concept than the urban place. An SMSA consists of one central city (or, in a few cases, more) with a population of at least 50,000 and of surrounding counties that are metropolitan in character. SMSA statistics thus do not require data from subdivisions smaller than counties, and the statistics are relatively plentiful. The most meaningful urban concept is the urbanized area, which is the urbanized part of the SMSA. But urbanized area statistics require data pertaining to areas smaller than counties, and they are thus not plentiful. In 1960, there were 212 SMSAs.

Table 2 shows the number and percentage of people living in SMSAs in census years since 1940. The similarity between corresponding figures in tables 1 and 2 is striking. Virtually the same number of people lived in SMSAs and in urban places in 1940, 1950, and 1960. Many people are included in both figures, since a large fraction of those who live in urban places also live in SMSAs. But some urban places, mostly small, are outside SMSAs. And some SMSA residents are rural and hence do not live in an urban place. These last two groups of people are similar in number, and hence SMSAs and urban places contain almost equal numbers of people.

Despite the similarity in numbers, the SMSA data provide a better picture of the metropolitan character of the United States than do the urban population data. Furthermore, they are not affected by the change in definition that makes the most recent urban data difficult to compare with earlier data. Since 1940 there has been a remarkably steady growth of between 3.9 and 4.9 percentage points per decade in the percentage of the population living in SMSAs. It would be interesting to compare this record with metropolitan growth in the nineteenth century to test whether

2. I am indebted to Irving Hoch for many suggestions on the subject of this paragraph.

Table 2. Population of United States and SMSAs, 1940–70

(population figures in millions)

Year	U.S. population	SMSA population	SMSA population as percent of U.S. population
1940	131.7	72.8	55.3
1950	150.7	89.3	59.3
1960	178.5	112.9	63.2
1970	203.2	136.3	67.1

Sources: U.S. Census of Population, 1960, 1970.

it displays the deceleration observed in the urban data. But the data are not available.

2. URBANIZATION OF EMPLOYMENT

SMSAs are, to a considerable extent, labor market areas. The amount of commuting to the central city is a major criterion in deciding to include a county in the SMSA. And, since most SMSAs include a considerable amount of rural land near their outer edges, few SMSA workers have reason to live beyond the edge of the SMSA. Therefore, almost by definition, the number of workers employed in SMSAs is nearly the same as the number of workers living in SMSAs. In fact, there is some commuting between SMSAs. For example, some people live in Gary and work in Chicago, live in Newark and work in New York, or live in Washington and work in Baltimore. But to live outside an SMSA and work in an SMSA is likely to be less common than to live in one SMSA and work in another. It follows that data on the numbers of workers resident in SMSAs will be an accurate guide to the numbers of workers employed in SMSAs. The 1960 census showed that, of all workers living in SMSAs, only 4 percent worked outside the SMSA in which they lived. And some of this small group worked in other SMSAs. It is thus not necessary to distinguish between place of residence and place of work in discussing SMSA employment. In section 5, where central city and suburban locations will be discussed, the distinction will be crucial.

It should be expected that some industries are predominantly located in SMSAs, whereas others are predominantly outside SMSAs. Table 3 shows U.S. and SMSA employment in twelve industry groups. The groups are exhaustive, including all employees except those who did not report industry of employment. The SMSAs included in table 3 are all those with at least 250,000 people. They will be referred to as large SMSAs. In 1960, 100 out of the 212 SMSAs were in this category. In 1950, just over half of all employees lived in large SMSAs. In 1960, 56.5 percent did.

Table 3. *Industry Groups of Employed Persons: United States and SMSAs with at least 250,000 Population, 1950 and 1960*

(*employment figures in thousands*)

Industry	1950 U.S.		1950 SMSAs		1950 Percent in SMSAs	1960 U.S.		1960 SMSAs		1960 Percent in SMSAs
	Number	Percent	Number	Percent		Number	Percent	Number	Percent	
Agriculture, forestry, fisheries	7,034	12.5	564	2.0	8.0	4,350	6.7	559	1.5	12.9
Mining	931	1.6	216	0.8	23.2	654	1.0	157	0.4	24.0
Construction	3,458	6.1	1,709	6.0	49.4	3,816	5.9	2,028	5.6	53.1
Manufacturing	14,685	26.0	8,676	30.6	59.1	17,513	27.1	10,643	29.1	60.8
Transportation, communication, utilities	4,450	7.9	2,551	9.0	57.3	4,458	6.9	2,764	7.6	62.0
Wholesaling, retailing	10,507	18.6	5,936	20.9	56.5	11,793	18.2	6,862	18.8	58.2
Finance, insurance, real estate	1,920	3.4	1,358	4.8	70.7	2,695	4.2	1,930	5.3	71.6
Business & repair services	1,308	2.3	784	2.8	59.9	1,610	2.5	1,057	2.9	65.7
Personal services	3,465	6.1	1,811	6.4	52.4	3,859	6.0	2,032	5.6	52.7
Entertainment, recreation	493	0.9	355	1.3	72.0	503	0.8	330	0.9	65.6
Professional services	4,826	8.6	2,489	8.8	51.6	7,578	11.7	4,345	11.9	57.3
Public administration	2,514	4.5	1,523	5.4	60.6	3,203	5.0	2,024	5.5	63.2
Not reported	843	1.5	371	1.3	44.0	2,608	4.0	1,788	4.9	68.6
Total	56,435	100.0	28,351	100.0	50.2	64,639	100.0	36,520	100.0	56.5

Sources: U.S. Census of Population, 1950, 1960.

Note: Numbers may not add to totals because of rounding.

The right-hand column for each year shows the percentage of all employees in each industry who lived in large SMSAs. In 1960, the percentages ranged from less than 13 to more than 71. The percentage in agriculture, not surprisingly, is the smallest, whereas that in finance, insurance, and real estate is the largest. Although manufacturing is the largest employer both in the United States and in large SMSAs, it is not, contrary to some popular writing, among the industries most concentrated in large SMSAs. In 1960, there were five industries in which a larger percentage of employment was in large SMSAs than was true in manufacturing. Manufacturing was only slightly more concentrated in large SMSAs than total employment. One of the surprises in table 3 is that construction is less concentrated in large SMSAs than total employment. One might have guessed that, since SMSAs are growing faster than the country as a whole, a larger percentage of construction workers than of all employees would be found in large SMSAs. But that is not the case. Part of the reason for the small concentration of construction in large SMSAs may be that military construction and the construction of the interstate highway system are concentrated in rural areas.

From 1950 to 1960, the total of employees living in large SMSAs increased by 6 percentage points. Perhaps surprisingly, the part of agricultural employment in large SMSAs rose from 8 to almost 13 percent. The increase results from a combination of a drop in total agricultural employment from 7.0 million to 4.4 million and a relatively small drop in agricultural employment in large SMSAs from 564 thousand to 559 thousand. A conjecture is that land prices in the rural parts of large SMSAs rose faster than wage rates and prices of other agricultural inputs, so SMSA agriculture became increasingly labor-intensive. There may also have been a tendency to substitute the production of labor-intensive agricultural products, such as dairy products, for that of other agricultural products near large population centers. The percentage of employment in large SMSAs remained about constant in mining, manufacturing, and several service industries. It rose substantially in transportation, communication, and utilities, in business and repair services, and in professional services. The figures undoubtedly reflect a general tendency to concentrate many kinds of service activities in large metropolitan areas. One reason is presumably that as service industries become more specialized, they find it increasingly advantageous to locate near related service establishments such as hospitals, courts, laboratories, and universities. Another probable reason is that improved transportation and communication have increased the ability of the service industry to provide services to customers whose residences are far away. A mystery in table 3 is the decrease in the percentage of entertainment and recreational employment found in large SMSAs. Possibly, increasing real incomes have induced SMSA residents to spend more of their leisure time outside SMSAs. In summary, the data in table 3 provide documentation that the growth of population in SMSAs since World War II has been related to the growth of employment in services, not in manufacturing.

Table 4 provides more detailed data concerning urbanization within manufacturing industry. The SMSAs included in table 4 are all those with at least 40,000 manufacturing employees. It is roughly the SMSAs that were included in table 3, but a few are included in each table that

Table 4. Manufacturing Employment in United States and in Large SMSAs by Standard Industrial Classification Industry Groups, 1947 and 1963

(*employment figures in thousands*)

SIC Code	Industry	1947			1963		
		U.S. employment	SMSA employment	Percent in SMSAs	U.S. employment	SMSA employment	Percent in SMSAs
20	Food	1,442	717	49.7	1,643	858	52.2
21	Tobacco	112	33	29.5	77	25	32.5
22	Textiles	1,233	384	31.1	863	233	27.0
23	Apparel	1,082	759	70.1	1,280	745	58.2
24	Lumber products	636	87	13.7	563	98	17.4
25	Furniture	322	158	49.1	377	181	48.0
26	Paper	450	207	46.0	588	286	48.6
27	Printing	715	511	71.5	913	658	72.1
28	Chemicals	632	370	58.5	737	411	55.8
29	Petroleum refining	212	133	62.7	153	75	49.0
30	Rubber products	259	176	68.0	415	260	62.7
31	Leather	383	159	41.5	327	143	43.7
32	Stone, clay, glass products	462	203	43.9	574	258	44.9
33	Primary metals	1,157	839	72.5	1,127	687	61.0
34	Fabricated metals	971	698	71.9	1,082	751	69.4
35	Nonelectrical machinery	1,545	1,018	65.9	1,459	958	65.7
36	Electrical machinery	801	614	76.7	1,512	1,029	68.1
37	Transportation equipment	1,182	901	76.2	1,601	1,170	73.1
38	Instruments	232	184	79.3	305	225	73.8
39	Miscellaneous	464	339	73.1	391	278	71.1
	Total	14,294	8,490	59.4	15,987	9,329	58.4

Sources: Compiled from data in U.S. Census of Manufactures, 1947, 1963.
Note: Numbers may not add to totals because of rounding.

are not in the other. The data in table 4 come from figures in the Census of Manufactures, which are available at five-year intervals from 1947 to 1963. The table shows employment in the United States and in these large SMSAs in each of the twenty two-digit[3] manufacturing industries.

Not surprisingly, some two-digit industries are much more urbanized than others. In 1963, large SMSA employment ranged from a low of 17.4 percent of total employment in lumber production to a high of 73.8 percent in scientific and technical instrument manufacture. Generally, the manufacturing industries least concentrated in large SMSAs are those whose major material inputs originate in rural areas. Food processing, tobacco products, textiles, lumber products, furniture, paper, chemicals, petroleum refining, leather, and stone, clay, and glass products are in this category. The most urbanized industries tend to be those in which material inputs have gone through several processing stages. Printing, fabricated metals, machinery, transportation equipment, and instruments fall in this category. The pattern is in keeping with classical notions of location theory, which lead us to expect industries engaged in early stages of fabrication to locate near raw material sources, and industries engaged in later stages of fabrication to locate near markets for their products and near large pools of skilled labor. An exception to the generalization is that primary metals manufacturing was somewhat more concentrated in large SMSAs than fabricated metals manufacturing in 1947. In 1963, the ranking was reversed.

Table 4 shows a drop of one percentage point, in the later year, in the percentage of manufacturing employment that is in large SMSAs. This finding is in contrast with that in table 3, which showed a slight increase in the percentage of manufacturing employment that is in large SMSAs. Both the years shown and the set of SMSAs included differ slightly between the two tables. There may have been a shift of manufacturing employment out of large SMSAs between 1960 and 1963. More likely is a shift during the entire postwar period toward SMSAs with relatively few manufacturing employees. Table 3 includes all SMSAs with at least 250,000 population, whereas table 4 includes only SMSAs with at least 40,000 manufacturing employees. In any case, the discrepancy is small.

If we consider the increases and decreases in concentration of manufacturing industries in large SMSAs, an interesting pattern emerges. The percentage of employment that was in large SMSAs fell in most two-digit industries and in those employing the most manufacturing workers. The percentage fell in thirteen of the twenty two-digit industries. In 1947,

3. On the basis of the Standard Industrial Classification Code.

the thirteen industries employed 69.5 percent of manufacturing workers in large SMSAs and 70.6 percent of manufacturing workers in the country. Thus, there was a pervasive and substantial decrease in the concentration of most manufacturing industries in large SMSAs. The reason that the result was only a slight decrease in the concentration of total manufacturing employment in large SMSAs is that there was a shift of employment in the direction of manufacturing industries that are concentrated in large SMSAs. In 1947, 39.7 percent of manufacturing employees were in two-digit industries whose concentration in large SMSAs was below the national average of 59.4 percent. By 1963, these industries employed only 36.0 percent of manufacturing employees. Although it did not happen, it is obviously possible for every two-digit industry to become less concentrated in SMSAs during a period in which all manufacturing industry becomes more concentrated in SMSAs.

The shift in employment toward industries concentrated in SMSAs is part of a pervasive shift toward industries engaged in later stages of fabrication. Increases in the amount of fabrication through which raw materials go before they reach the final consumer are an almost inevitable characteristic of technical progress. Indeed, the industrial revolution, which largely created urban society, was part of that process. The same phenomenon probably explains the tendency toward increased concentration in SMSAs in those little-urbanized industries engaged in early stages of fabrication. That is, the number of stages of fabrication has probably increased within two-digit industries. As a result, some parts of the two-digit industry have become less tied to raw material sources.

Another interesting characteristic of the data in table 4 is that decreases in SMSA concentration are most common in the two-digit industries most concentrated in SMSAs. Of the five industries with the largest SMSA concentration in 1947, all were less concentrated by 1963. It is also true that increases in SMSA concentration were most common in the industries that were least concentrated in SMSAs in 1947. Of the five least concentrated industries in 1947, four were more concentrated by 1963. This suggests that the pattern may be nothing more than the familiar phenomenon of regression toward the mean. If there is a random influence on the data, those observations that are above average in one period are likely to decrease by the next period, and those that are below average are likely to increase. But it is likely that there is an additional explanation at least for the decreased SMSA concentration of the most concentrated industries. As real incomes rise, the market becomes large enough to support certain industries in urban areas that were previously too small to support those industries. But neither explanation is more than speculation. More research is needed on the issue.

There are of course special explanations for the observed changes in particular industries. The decreased concentration of textile manufacturing in SMSAs is part of the migration of this industry from New England to predominantly rural parts of the South, which has been extensively studied. Decreased concentration of apparel manufacturing in SMSAs is presumably strongly influenced by its movement out of New York City. Decreased SMSA concentrations in petroleum refining, rubber products, and primary metals may be partly explained by increasingly stringent antipollution regulations in SMSAs. But changes in electrical machinery, transportation equipment, and instruments manufacturing are harder to explain.

Thus, the pattern since World War II has been increased SMSA concentration of two-digit manufacturing industries engaged in early stages of fabrication, decreased concentration in many industries engaged in later stages of fabrication, and a shift of employment from the former to the latter. It will be interesting to see whether this pattern continues during coming years.

3. Specialization Among SMSAs

Even if all metropolitan areas were completely autarkic, they would have somewhat different patterns of production resulting from differences in tastes, incomes, size, and factor prices. But metropolitan areas are by no means autarkic, and we should expect considerable specialization among them. In fact, a great deal has been written about specialization among metropolitan areas, cities, and regions, especially in relation to size. The most elaborate study is that by Duncan and others [7]. Although such studies contain much useful data and analysis, hardly any of them present comprehensive data on the simplest measures of dispersion of employment or production. Some measures of this kind are presented and analyzed in this section.

Tables 5 and 6 present the percentage distribution of employment by industry in a sample of large SMSAs for 1950 and 1960. The samples were drawn by taking every fifth entry in alphabetical lists of all SMSAs with at least 250,000 people. The SMSAs from which the samples were drawn are therefore those on which table 3 is based. In 1950, the list included 77 SMSAs, and in 1960 it included 100. The 1950 sample consisted of 16 SMSAs; the 1960 sample, 20. Seven SMSAs appear in both samples. That the samples of SMSAs are broadly representative of the list of all large SMSAs is shown by the last two lines of tables 5 and 6. The last line in each table shows the percentage distribution of employment in all large SMSAs; it is the same as the corresponding percent column in table 3. The next-to-last rows in tables 5 and 6 show the percentage

distribution of employment in the two 20-percent samples. The distributions in the samples and in the lists of all large SMSAs are quite similar,
as should be expected.

Tables 5 and 6 clearly show that the percentage of the labor force in
various industries differs considerably among SMSAs. The variability is,
however, considerably less than one would expect from the elaborate
classifications of urban areas by functional types that have appeared in
the literature. In 1950, manufacturing varied from a low of 7.8 percent
of employment in the Miami SMSA to a high of 55.8 percent in Flint.
Employment in finance, insurance, and real estate varied from 2.2 percent
to 12.1 percent of SMSA employment. In professional services, the range
was only from 6.1 percent to 10.5 percent.

However, the expected value of the sample range depends on sample
size as well as on other things, and it is desirable to choose a measure of
dispersion that is independent of sample size. Table 7 shows the standard
deviations of the distributions in tables 5 and 6. Each entry in table 7 is
the unweighted standard deviation of the corresponding column in table
5 or 6. The standard deviation decreased in all three industries that had
the largest SMSA employment in 1950. Of the seven industries that
employed at least 5 percent of all large SMSA employees in 1950, the
standard deviation of employment decreased in five industries between
1950 and 1960.

Thus, the sample standard deviations indicate that between 1950
and 1960 there was a decrease in specialization among SMSAs with at
least 250,000 population. Indeed, it would be surprising if it were otherwise. On almost any hypothesis, large SMSAs should be less specialized
than small SMSAs. And the average size of SMSAs with at least 250,000
population was greater in 1960 than in 1950. The 1950 sample had an
average of 255,000 employees per SMSA, whereas the 1960 sample had
an average of 452,000.

A more interesting question is whether specialization has increased
among SMSAs in a given size class. To answer this question, standard
deviations similar to those in table 7 were calculated for all the SMSAs in
tables 5 and 6 that had no more than 250,000 employees. The data are in
table 8. The entries in table 8 are standard deviations of those numbers
in corresponding columns of tables 5 and 6 that pertain to SMSAs with
no more than 250,000 employees. Thus, table 8 shows the standard deviations of the percentage distribution of employment for a sample of SMSAs
with at least 250,000 population and no more than 250,000 employees.
The sample size is 10 for 1950 and 13 for 1960.

Table 8 shows the same tendency toward decreased specialization
among these medium-sized SMSAs that was observed in the larger sample.
Of the twelve industries, standard deviations decreased in eight, increased

Table 5. Percentage of Employment in Industry Groups for Selected SMSAs, 1950

SMSA	Total employed	Agri-culture, forestry, fishing	Mining	Con-struction	Manu-facturing	Transpor-tation, commu-nication, public utilities
Akron	158,443	1.0	0.1	4.1	48.8	6.4
Birmingham	201,512	1.4	8.0	6.0	26.0	9.3
Charleston, W.Va.	104,879	1.8	19.9	5.8	22.4	8.2
Dallas	268,092	1.6	1.2	9.5	18.6	9.8
Flint	108,525	2.3	0.1	3.5	55.8	4.0
Hartford	156,263	2.3	0.1	5.4	32.8	4.5
Kansas City	339,811	2.3	0.2	6.6	23.9	12.6
Miami	199,892	2.9	0.1	10.6	7.8	11.1
New Orleans	254,838	1.1	0.8	7.3	15.7	14.7
Peoria	100,681	5.5	0.6	5.7	38.3	7.5
Providence	293,011	1.3	0.0	5.2	46.8	5.5
St. Louis	676,917	2.0	0.4	5.2	33.8	10.1
San Francisco	864,567	2.0	0.1	7.1	20.0	10.8
Syracuse	138,069	2.9	0.1	5.1	35.3	8.2
Utica-Rome	106,796	7.2	0.1	4.4	38.7	6.4
Worcester	104,705	1.3	0.0	4.8	43.3	5.9
Total sample	4,077,001	2.1	1.2	6.4	28.6	9.5
Total SMSAs	28,347,527	2.0	0.8	6.0	30.6	9.0

in three, and remained constant in one. Furthermore, the decreases in standard deviations are again most common in the industries with the largest employment. Standard deviations decreased between 1950 and 1960 in all three industries with the largest employment in 1950, and in five of the seven industries that employed at least 5 percent of all employees.

The samples thus indicate that not only large SMSAs but also SMSAs within a particular size class are becoming less specialized. Decreased specialization is presumably to be accounted for at least in part by rising real incomes. Rising real incomes cause growth in markets served by metropolitan areas of given population. As markets grow, production can take place in metropolitan areas previously unable to support the activity.

4. SUBURBANIZATION OF POPULATION AND EMPLOYMENT

Suburbanization is one of the most extensively discussed urban phenomena of our time. For reasons probably more comprehensible to the

Whole-saling, retailing	Finance, insurance, real estate	Business & repair services	Personal services	Enter-tainment, recreation	Profes-sional services	Public adminis-tration	Not reported
18.0	2.6	2.3	4.9	1.0	7.2	2.6	0.9
20.6	4.0	1.9	10.7	0.7	7.7	2.8	0.8
18.7	2.2	1.9	5.7	0.8	7.5	3.6	1.4
25.9	6.9	3.2	9.3	1.4	7.2	4.0	1.1
16.2	2.2	1.6	4.1	0.9	6.1	1.9	1.4
19.7	12.1	2.4	5.0	0.7	9.6	4.6	0.9
24.0	5.3	2.8	6.3	1.1	8.2	4.9	1.9
27.9	5.3	3.6	14.6	2.3	8.3	4.1	1.3
25.5	4.5	2.8	9.5	1.8	9.5	5.8	1.1
20.0	3.1	2.3	4.8	0.9	7.8	2.5	1.1
17.6	3.1	2.1	4.2	0.9	7.4	4.5	1.3
20.4	4.1	2.4	6.0	0.9	7.9	5.0	1.9
22.9	6.2	3.2	6.9	1.3	10.2	8.0	1.2
20.6	4.0	2.4	5.3	1.0	10.2	4.0	0.9
17.6	2.9	2.1	4.8	0.8	10.0	4.0	1.0
18.9	3.6	2.1	4.5	0.6	10.5	3.4	0.9
21.7	4.9	2.6	6.9	1.1	8.6	5.0	1.3
20.9	4.8	2.8	6.4	1.3	8.8	5.4	1.3

Source: U.S. Census of Population, 1950.
Note: Percentages may not add to 100 because of rounding.

social psychologist than to the economist, the subject arouses strong emotions on all sides. But, as with other contemporary social issues, the highly charged adversary discourse bears little relationship to the rather prosaic phenomenon.

In any reasonable definition, suburbanization is an inevitable concomitant of urban growth. There are many interesting questions to ask about suburbanization, of which the following three are among the more significant. First, how should suburbanization be measured and what is its magnitude? Second, is there reason to believe that the pattern or mechanism of suburbanization has changed since World War II? Third, what are the basic causes of the process? Much of the rest of this book is devoted to one aspect or another of these questions. In this section, attention is devoted primarily to the factual basis of suburbanization.

As with other urban data, the major sources of comprehensive information concerning suburbanization are the various United States censuses. Although the Census of Population gives data on the industry of

Table 6. Percentage of Employment in Industry Groups for Selected SMSAs, 1960

SMSA	Total employed	Agri- culture, forestry, fishing	Mining	Con- struction	Manu- facturing	Transpor- tation, commu- nication, public utilities
Akron	188,960	0.7	0.1	4.1	44.7	6.7
Bakersfield	98,273	15.2	5.5	6.4	9.8	7.0
Bridgeport	132,443	0.5	0.0	5.4	45.8	4.5
Chattanooga	103,495	1.8	0.2	5.4	34.6	6.5
Columbus, Ohio	256,684	1.0	0.3	6.0	26.2	7.0
Des Moines	107,563	2.3	0.1	5.4	21.2	7.9
Flint	132,406	1.2	0.0	3.4	50.7	4.0
Grand Rapids	132,239	2.1	0.2	5.1	36.2	6.3
Huntington- Ashland	80,302	2.2	1.1	6.3	29.8	11.0
Kansas City	407,343	1.2	0.2	5.2	24.6	10.8
Louisville	255,505	1.5	0.1	5.8	31.3	8.4
Mobile	106,211	2.2	0.3	6.9	17.2	9.0
New York	4,372,640	0.4	0.1	4.5	25.8	8.5
Peoria	108,050	3.5	0.2	5.3	36.5	6.7
Providence	313,663	1.0	0.0	5.1	42.1	4.5
St. Louis	763,637	1.3	0.3	4.9	33.0	8.5
San Francisco	1,076,002	1.4	0.2	5.7	21.0	9.1
Springfield, Mass.	178,856	1.1	0.0	4.1	39.6	5.2
Trenton	108,786	1.3	0.1	6.1	32.0	5.4
Wichita	126,416	1.8	1.2	5.0	32.3	6.2
Total sample	9,049,474	1.0	0.2	4.9	28.1	8.1
Total SMSAs	36,519,967	1.5	0.4	5.6	29.1	7.6

employees by place of residence for census tracts, industry of employees by place of employment is available only for the dichotomous classifica- tion of SMSAs into central cities and suburban rings. Although the di- chotomy is somewhat crude, it is sufficiently detailed for many purposes. An alternative approach, using some of the same data, is employed in the next chapter.

The major problem with the central city–suburban ring dichotomy is that the boundaries of the central city change through time, mainly through the annexation of adjacent suburbs. Annexation was common among East Coast industrial cities during the nineteenth century and continues, mainly in the West, in the twentieth. It is possible to make an approximate correction for annexations between 1950 and 1960, but not for earlier years. The method of correction is given in Niedercorn and

Whole-saling, retailing	Finance, insurance, real estate	Business & repair services	Personal services	Enter-tainment, recreation	Profes-sional services	Public adminis-tration	Not reported
17.0	3.2	2.3	4.4	0.8	10.6	2.6	2.8
18.7	3.4	3.0	6.1	0.9	11.9	9.2	3.1
15.3	3.2	2.1	3.5	0.5	9.9	3.2	6.1
17.2	4.8	2.3	7.8	0.6	10.3	4.0	4.5
19.0	5.3	2.5	5.6	0.7	15.5	6.7	4.2
21.8	9.6	3.0	5.4	0.8	13.0	6.1	3.5
16.4	2.6	1.6	4.3	0.5	10.1	2.2	3.1
20.4	4.2	2.9	5.3	0.6	11.8	2.6	2.4
19.7	3.1	1.9	5.8	0.6	11.5	3.3	3.6
20.8	5.8	2.6	5.2	0.8	11.2	5.2	6.4
18.9	4.5	2.1	5.8	0.8	11.3	4.3	5.3
19.6	3.9	2.0	10.2	0.6	10.5	15.5	2.0
19.0	7.7	3.8	5.8	1.1	12.4	4.8	6.1
19.0	3.9	2.0	4.4	0.6	11.1	2.7	4.0
16.0	3.5	2.0	3.5	0.7	10.6	5.3	5.6
17.9	4.7	2.4	5.1	0.7	11.0	4.7	5.6
19.0	6.7	3.6	6.0	1.0	13.9	7.2	5.3
17.9	4.8	1.9	3.7	0.6	12.6	4.2	4.3
14.8	3.1	3.3	4.9	0.5	15.9	8.4	4.1
19.8	4.9	2.4	5.2	0.7	12.4	4.3	3.7
18.7	6.3	3.2	5.6	0.9	12.3	5.2	5.4
18.8	5.3	2.9	5.6	0.9	11.9	5.5	4.9

Source: U.S. Census of Population, 1960.
Note: Percentages may not add to 100 because of rounding.

Kain [29]. All the data used in this section and presented in appendix table 2–1 at the end of this chapter have been adjusted to 1950 central city boundaries.

The most readily available employment data are those from the Censuses of Manufactures and Business. Coverage of Census of Manufactures data was discussed in the previous section. Among the exhaustive set of industries included in tables 5 and 6, the Census of Business presents data for retailing, wholesaling, and selected services. The last category includes roughly the following major industry groups: finance, insurance, and real estate; business and repair services; personal services; and enter-tainment and recreational services. Thus, the only substantial urban em-

Table 7. Standard Deviations of Employment in Industry Groups Among Sample SMSAs, 1950 and 1960

Industry group	Standard deviations	
	1950	1960
Agriculture, etc.	1.6	3.0
Mining	4.9	1.1
Construction	1.8	0.8
Manufacturing	12.5	9.7
Transportation, etc.	2.8	1.9
Wholesaling, retailing	3.2	1.7
Finance, etc.	2.3	1.7
Business & repair services	0.4	0.6
Personal services	2.7	1.4
Entertainment	0.4	0.3
Professional services	1.0	1.6
Public services	1.4	2.9
Not reported	0.3	1.3

Source: Calculated from data in tables 5 and 6.

Table 8. Standard Deviations of Employment in Industry Groups for a Sample of SMSAs with no More Than 250,000 Employees

Industry group	Standard deviations	
	1950	1960
Agriculture, etc.	2.0	3.8
Mining	6.5	1.5
Construction	1.9	1.0
Manufacturing	14.0	11.6
Transportation, etc.	2.2	1.8
Wholesaling, retailing	3.2	2.0
Finance, etc.	2.9	1.8
Business & repair services	0.5	0.5
Personal services	3.4	1.8
Entertainment	0.5	0.3
Professional services	1.5	1.6
Public services	0.8	3.7
Not reported	0.3	1.0

Source: Calculated from data in tables 5 and 6.

ployees excluded from the data in this section are construction; transportation, communication, and public utilities; professional services; and public administration. Almost two-thirds of employment in the SMSAs studied is included in the data analyzed in this section.

Table 9 shows central city and suburban ring population and employment by place of employment for 90 SMSAs. The 90 SMSAs were obtained as follows. From the list of 100 SMSAs containing at least 250,000 people in 1960, on which the 1960 data in table 3 are based, the following

Table 9. *Suburbanization of Population and Employment in Ninety SMSAs, 1947–63*
(*population and employment figures in thousands*)

Sector	1947 or 1950				1960 or 1963			
	City		Ring		City		Ring	
	Num-ber	Per-cent	Num-ber	Per-cent	Num-ber	Per-cent	Num-ber	Per-cent
Population	26,742	53.0	23,506	47.0	26,554	40.0	39,483	60.0
Manufacturing employment	3,750	60.5	2,449	39.5	3,250	46.2	3,791	53.8
Retailing employment	2,032	71.5	811	28.5	1,667	48.7	1,756	51.3
Service employment	673	79.5	173	20.5	826	61.1	525	38.9
Wholesaling employment	980	85.2	171	14.8	943	65.2	503	34.8
Total employment	7,435	67.3	3,604	32.7	6,686	50.4	6,575	49.6

Sources: U.S. Census of Population, 1950 and 1960; U.S. Census of Business, 1948 and 1963; U.S. Census of Manufactures, 1948 and 1963.

Note: Numbers may not add to totals because of rounding.

SMSAs were removed: those comprising the New York–Northeastern New Jersey and Chicago–Northwestern Indiana Standard Consolidated Areas; the three contiguous SMSAs in the Los Angeles area; and Washington, D.C. The 10 SMSAs removed were New York, Jersey City, Newark, Paterson, Chicago, Gary, Los Angeles, Anaheim, San Bernardino, and Washington. The reason for removing the first nine is that the central cities of some of these SMSAs tend to be the suburbs of others. The reason for removing the tenth is that all the employment data in table 9 refer to the private sector and, in Washington, locational decisions are overwhelmingly affected by the federal government. These exclusions are of course somewhat arbitrary. Some readers would undoubtedly include some and exclude others. In fact, rough calculations suggest that the trends identified in this section are affected little if the ten excluded SMSAs are included.

The first columns of table 9 show population data for 1950 and employment data for 1947. The last columns show population data for 1960 and employment data for 1963. It should be noted that the data for the early postwar years pertain to all 90 SMSAs that had at least 250,000 population in 1960, not just to those whose population reached that level in the year in question. It seems desirable to measure suburbanization for the same set of SMSAs at all points in time. In 1960, the 90 SMSAs contained 37 percent of the country's population. Since the data underlying table 9 come from a variety of sources and represent a considerable amount of processing, the individual data for the 90 SMSAs are presented in appendix table 2–1 at the end of this chapter.

Not surprisingly, table 9 shows that population is more suburbanized than employment. In 1960, 60.0 percent of the population of the 90 SMSAs lived in the suburbs, whereas 49.6 percent of the employees worked in the suburbs. This simply shows that more people commute into central cities than out of them in the mornings. Within the employment category, the ranking of industries by degree of suburbanization remained unchanged during the postwar period. Manufacturing is the most suburbanized industry, then retailing, services, and wholesaling, in that order.

The magnitude of the postwar suburbanization indicated in table 9 is impressive indeed. Central city population fell from 53.0 percent of SMSA population in 1950 to 40.0 percent in 1960. Central city employment fell from 67.3 percent of SMSA employment in 1947 to 50.4 percent in 1963. Moreover, total central city population and employment fell slightly during the period covered by the table. In only one category, services, did central city employment increase between 1947 and 1963.

As measured in the table, population and manufacturing suburbanized least of all the sectors included. The percentage of the population living in suburbs went from 47.0 to 60.0, an increase of 13 percentage points. For manufacturing, the increase was 14.3 points. But for the other employment categories, the figures are: retailing, 22.8; services, 18.4; wholesaling, 20.0. Some popular writing gives the impression that suburbanization has occurred mainly among the residential population and manufacturing industry. But the measures presented here indicate the contrary. The employment data in table 9 cover a longer period than the population data. Therefore, the extent of suburbanization is not quite comparable.

Table 10 shows the average annual percentage growth rates of popu-

Table 10. Average Annual Growth Rates of Central Cities and Suburbs in Ninety SMSAs, 1947–63

(*in percent per year*)

Sector	Central cities	Suburbs	SMSAs
Population	−0.1	6.8	3.1
Manufacturing employment	−0.8	3.4	0.9
Retailing employment	−1.1	7.3	1.3
Service employment	+1.4	12.7	3.7
Wholesaling employment	−0.2	12.1	1.6
Total employment	−0.6	5.2	1.3

Source: Calculated from data in table 9.

lation and the employment categories in central cities, surbubs, and SMSAs. The data in table 10 are simple averages, not compounded. These data tell the same story about suburbanization as the data in table 9. The two slowest growing sectors in the suburbs were population and manufacturing employment. Service employment grew fastest, followed by wholesaling and retailing. As the last column in table 10 shows, total SMSA employment grew fastest in services, whereas manufacturing was the slowest growing sector.

Appendix Table 2–1. Suburbanization of Population and Employment in Ninety SMSAs, 1948–63

SMSA	Population				Manufacturing			
	1950		1960		1948		1963	
	City	Ring	City	Ring	City	Ring	City	Ring
Akron	274,605	135,427	289,822	223,747	76,534	17,477	58,538	32,142
Albany	134,905	379,495	129,726	527,777	10,499	60,340	6,995	54,754
Albuquerque	96,815	48,858	177,543	84,656	1,466	488	5,476	2,681
Allentown	106,756	331,068	107,922	384,246	24,204	64,335	24,934	68,817
Atlanta	331,314	340,483	315,988	701,200	36,172	12,862	31,648	64,048
Bakersfield	34,784	193,525	32,872	259,112	956	1,948	1,061	4,783
Baltimore	949,708	455,691	939,024	787,999	120,929	49,133	103,825	86,687
Beaumont	94,014	101,069	110,741	195,275	2,901	20,280	3,543	29,270
Birmingham	326,037	232,891	328,173	306,691	26,484	26,811	32,097	27,261
Boston	801,444	1,567,540	697,197	1,893,280	101,722	169,643	82,512	210,729
Bridgeport	158,709	99,428	156,748	177,828	54,976	15,151	36,834	30,585
Buffalo	580,132	509,098	532,759	774,198	87,279	96,597	57,047	105,895
Canton	116,912	166,282	113,600	226,745	32,835	22,729	23,169	29,793
Charleston, W.Va.	73,501	248,574	67,111	185,814	2,426	23,495	4,423	16,734
Charlotte	134,052	63,000	144,858	127,253	13,515	4,685	15,683	17,072
Chattanooga	131,041	115,412	120,576	162,593	30,572	7,621	25,736	13,204
Cincinnati	503,998	400,404	502,550	765,929	97,511	38,263	76,624	77,306
Cleveland	914,808	550,703	876,050	1,033,430	223,641	45,109	168,875	111,410
Columbia. S.C.	62,396	42,447	97,443	163,395	3,656	3,434	6,348	8,117
Columbus, Ohio	375,901	127,509	395,681	287,281	41,367	13,510	52,154	28,085
Dallas	434,462	130,337	486,977	596,624	34,245	4,691	58,185	51,332
Davenport	74,549	159,707	80,423	189,735	6,928	30,363	7,010	34,076
Dayton	243,872	213,461	229,560	497,561	75,843	19,504	67,974	36,215
Denver	415,786	148,046	455,604	473,734	30,876	3,371	34,111	35,428
Des Moines	177,965	48,045	190,045	76,270	14,088	2,002	13,304	8,317
Detroit	1,849,570	1,166,630	1,670,140	2,092,220	333,373	217,415	200,586	293,327
Duluth	104,511	148,266	106,884	169,712	110,424	2,507	7,936	3,586
El Paso	130,485	64,483	152,532	161,538	5,028	1,148	7,342	7,574
Erie	130,803	83,077	138,440	112,242	24,976	21,309	20,247	16,190
Flint	163,143	107,820	196,940	177,373	53,770	1,389	46,531	22,344
Ft. Lauderdale	36,328	47,605	77,008	256,938	588	196	3,347	6,403
Ft. Worth	278,778	82,475	256,268	316,947	30,495	1,544	32,884	17,650
Fresno	91,669	184,846	89,362	276,583	3,283	4,236	3,487	10,822
Grand Rapids	176,515	111,777	176,658	186,529	44,179	5,062	34,400	30,202
Harrisburg	89,544	202,697	79,697	265,374	8,670	22,214	8,858	24,612
Hartford	177,397	180,684	162,178	363,029	34,536	29,256	2,232	67,945
Houston	596,163	210,538	687,026	731,297	40,563	18,043	53,432	55,153
Huntington	86,358	159,437	83,197	171,583	9,896	12,291	9,247	14,351
Indianapolis	427,173	124,604	428,809	268,758	79,805	12,844	61,140	54,677
Jacksonville	204,517	99,512	201,030	254,381	12,221	550	16,139	4,447
Johnstown	63,232	228,122	53,949	233,381	20,170	3,182	15,889	7,134
Kansas City	456,622	357,735	433,521	659,024	46,683	31,962	54,954	56,150
Knoxville	124,769	212,336	111,827	656,253	19,273	11,920	20,210	14,644
Lancaster	63,774	170,943	59,881	218,478	16,617	22,090	17,695	30,183
Lansing	92,129	80,812	96,041	202,908	24,898	954	20,601	7,780
Louisville	369,129	207,771	328,410	396,729	55,575	18,216	45,967	41,654
Memphis	396,000	86,393	428,429	198,590	33,160	2,056	35,092	12,060
Miami	249,276	245,808	291,688	643,359	7,086	2,185	19,214	24,031
Milwaukee	637,392	233,655	617,454	615,277	133,051	44,151	93,373	100,472
Minneapolis	521,718	594,791	482,872	1,000,160	61,942	56,882	67,031	96,789
Mobile	129,009	102,096	140,404	173,897	8,337	9,244	9,544	9,007
Nashville	174,307	147,451	163,597	236,146	21,726	8,584	32,149	14,370
New Haven	164,443	100,179	152,048	159,633	33,461	8,042	29,734	13,263
New Orleans	570,445	114,960	627,525	240,955	35,302	10,061	31,054	17,997
Norfolk	213,513	232,687	217,551	360,956	10,336	6,457	7,669	8,405
Oklahoma City	243,504	81,821	254,077	257,756	8,566	4,707	17,526	9,718
Omaha	251,117	115,278	261,382	196,491	25,399	2,159	22,485	12,597
Orlando	52,367	92,583	69,634	248,853	1,717	1,035	3,622	15,767
Peoria	111,856	133,956	100,933	187,900	13,652	28,859	10,549	29,538
Philadelphia	2,071,600	1,590,440	2,002,510	2,341,010	328,630	203,862	264,893	270,914

	Retailing				Services				Wholesaling		
1948		1963		1948		1963		1948		1963	
City	Ring	City	Ring	City	Ring	City	Ring	City	Ring	City	Ring
18,310	4,460	15,981	12,947	4,763	981	5,816	2,749	4,445	699	6,397	2,329
10,657	20,007	9,574	23,601	4,166	3,956	4,490	9,856	4,779	3,746	5,185	6,253
6,366	327	11,520	3,061	2,093	49	4,296	1,024	1,929	215	4,125	1,333
9,395	12,925	9,345	14,544	2,169	2,817	2,989	3,387	2,909	2,909	3,523	3,364
35,318	8,501	24,594	34,538	13,209	2,314	14,168	14,429	25,420	3,185	19,960	21,865
5,542	4,248	3,516	10,997	1,711	999	1,439	3,487	1,596	1,433	1,172	2,532
69,230	8,724	57,193	35,760	20,790	2,106	24,941	10,005	26,209	1,380	26,629	5,066
6,702	4,191	5,838	7,234	1,992	1,008	2,551	2,214	2,128	356	2,753	1,450
22,213	5,292	19,644	7,812	8,081	1,319	8,433	2,248	11,590	981	12,791	1,936
74,310	72,553	55,974	98,140	25,434	17,354	31,985	29,359	46,337	17,330	33,195	31,618
11,017	2,319	9,279	7,480	3,028	512	3,244	1,742	3,173	627	4,951	1,492
40,927	18,355	28,914	33,836	12,555	3,324	12,630	8,753	17,388	2,705	15,319	6,286
9,046	6,215	6,989	8,675	2,568	997	2,406	1,863	2,687	908	2,909	1,816
8,786	5,805	5,478	5,197	2,819	840	2,038	1,397	4,231	321	2,671	1,494
10,599	927	9,587	7,305	3,995	176	6,053	3,673	8,124	821	10,207	6,251
10,542	1,464	8,569	4,545	4,047	504	3,941	1,754	3,679	193	4,482	847
38,622	16,012	31,060	27,550	15,835	2,700	16,422	6,261	20,574	3,308	20,177	6,630
68,888	19,326	46,974	47,181	24,894	3,822	26,765	13,147	36,841	2,843	33,226	11,987
7,262	596	7,651	3,351	2,665	140	3,593	1,161	2,955	219	3,909	' 960
28,988	3,425	23,338	18,030	9,824	405	10,845	5,482	9,777	1,364	10,031	5,278
37,000	5,923	33,435	32,610	12,042	320	19,061	12,325	25,197	1,327	27,009	15,689
6,639	8,019	5,357	12,563	1,961	1,721	1,912	3,089	1,941	2,202	2,025	3,229
21,754	5,567	16,485	20,329	5,275	1,159	6,356	5,297	5,695	392	6,137	3,649
31,651	3,705	30,377	26,046	10,651	724	16,317	7,369	19,222	424	19,938	5,571
14,467	1,238	13,684	3,278	4,872	196	5,628	1,180	7,553	416	7,324	1,545
114,038	48,124	72,149	93,668	46,796	7,374	46,838	24,223	45,079	7,556	44,615	20,393
6,777	6,041	5,931	5,558	1,500	1,500	1,787	1,265	4,054	1,682	2,801	1,380
9,158	1,067	7,640	7,420	2,656	444	2,811	2,797	3,859	112	2,804	2,481
9,944	2,331	7,492	3,794	2,207	421	2,357	748	2,708	294	2,513	451
10,690	2,112	12,571	6,274	2,658	327	3,335	1,033	3,655	151	3,656	3,931
3,202	1,762	9,594	12,691	789	698	4,699	5,992	352	162	2,086	2,186
22,181	1,523	20,304	12,677	6,840	1,499	8,179	3,825	7,010	720	7,899	3,621
8,906	3,537	7,488	11,479	1,724	1,832	3,350	3,695	4,058	3,666	3,213	4,860
14,186	2,975	11,446	10,704	4,514	399	5,574	1,763	4,965	655	6,721	3,541
9,183	7,926	7,775	12,546	2,747	1,812	3,140	3,261	4,113	1,226	4,310	3,620
17,531	6,697	13,844	19,022	4,987	1,413	8,122	3,971	6,632	1,717	6,756	5,630
37,808	7,501	38,661	28,354	14,130	1,562	21,629	12,262	21,681	1,980	25,991	12,967
5,587	4,436	5,241	4,928	1,420	1,256	2,021	1,443	2,867	858	3,104	1,033
37,469	3,234	31,998	20,010	11,963	450	12,617	4,150	14,395	1,828	16,738	5,558
15,051	2,004	16,336	8,133	6,485	344	8,886	1,482	9,386	1,018	11,059	1,772
6,396	6,693	4,276	5,580	1,466	1,101	1,046	987	1,600	607	1,275	944
46,203	15,435	35,029	29,268	15,971	3,041	16,627	8,509	24,953	7,374	21,048	12,254
11,402	4,075	11,272	5,979	3,893	775	4,405	1,261	4,483	378	6,381	501
5,776	5,320	4,507	8,821	1,206	719	1,541	1,623	1,615	968	2,164	1,984
8,276	2,134	7,912	7,110	1,799	301	2,376	1,599	1,945	155	2,713	1,308
24,416	5,969	19,219	17,243	8,230	838	9,657	4,928	13,592	1,097	11,105	4,443
27,633	1,597	23,366	9,504	7,698	2,039	11,079	3,488	15,111	873	16,839	4,734
22,486	11,450	24,371	34,683	9,296	7,320	18,552	23,837	8,416	1,542	13,904	9,036
47,957	7,066	33,014	32,514	13,538	1,269	14,049	8,932	20,832	1,740	15,256	9,829
46,536	33,101	36,806	51,398	11,000	6,000	20,857	14,648	25,804	10,294	27,734	18,486
8,499	1,590	7,171	7,773	3,126	374	2,857	2,570	3,313	431	3,209	2,505
14,269	2,861	15,262	6,492	5,724	380	7,736	1,955	7,596	223	10,725	1,431
11,089	2,694	8,373	7,740	4,320	672	4,995	1,655	6,688	1,037	4,722	3,289
34,171	2,751	32,998	10,446	12,108	739	17,880	3,822	19,627	1,057	19,115	4,169
15,217	6,318	12,182	14,931	4,485	2,243	4,787	5,111	6,463	1,137	4,606	3,828
17,412	1,928	15,328	13,390	6,781	449	7,893	4,610	9,060	957	9,121	4,216
17,752	4,257	16,488	8,668	6,760	807	7,263	2,890	790	140	706	303
5,016	1,089	8,390	9,075	1,706	316	4,228	3,166	2,528	1,810	4,614	4,151
9,864	3,880	8,228	7,966	3,137	694	3,052	1,405	3,796	638	3,526	1,760
131,251	60,682	100,681	106,487	41,188	13,819	21,990	14,119	30,532	7,144	22,920	14,646

Appendix Table 2-1 (continued)

SMSA	Population				Manufacturing			
	1950		1960		1948		1963	
	City	Ring	City	Ring	City	Ring	City	Ring
Phoenix	106,818	224,952	106,772	556,738	3,024	4,425	6,592	34,378
Pittsburgh	676,806	1,536,430	604,322	1,801,160	81,415	256,559	81,707	190,476
Portland, Oreg.	373,628	331,201	361,663	460,234	33,803	17,840	34,277	30,988
Providence	248,674	488,529	207,498	613,606	61,230	76,194	41,501	84,385
Reading	109,320	146,420	98,177	177,237	27,111	26,312	21,504	29,125
Richmond	230,310	97,740	219,958	188,536	28,068	7,165	33,887	11,893
Rochester	332,488	155,144	318,611	413,977	99,934	5,063	97,345	23,999
Sacramento	137,572	139,568	138,995	368,783	5,716	2,604	4,612	30,660
St. Louis	856,796	824,485	750,062	1,354,610	172,946	71,570	129,060	130,617
Salt Lake City	182,121	92,774	185,989	197,046	7,940	2,909	16,783	15,002
San Antonio	408,442	92,018	448,226	238,925	14,411	1,103	15,827	7,777
San Diego	334,387	222,421	507,381	525,630	18,553	2,230	41,400	18,876
San Francisco	775,357	1,465,410	740,316	1,908,450	61,574	102,067	60,639	135,524
Seattle	467,591	265,401	471,008	636,205	50,214	4,556	63,372	58,184
Shreveport	127,026	89,660	129,131	152,350	4,504	3,275	5,281	3,830
Spokane	161,721	59,840	179,423	98,910	6,532	4,392	7,114	4,711
Springfield, Mass.	162,399	244,856	174,463	304,129	28,210	53,388	23,987	43,367
Syracuse	220,583	121,136	215,817	347,964	35,264	19,299	19,941	47,162
Tacoma	143,673	132,203	147,979	173,611	12,063	3,933	13,593	2,971
Tampa	124,681	284,462	134,639	637,814	14,417	3,707	8,281	28,679
Toledo	303,616	91,935	298,832	158,099	59,500	10,099	49,725	21,019
Trenton	128,000	101,772	114,167	152,225	30,323	10,099	17,660	20,129
Tucson	45,454	95,762	45,780	219,880	1,045	129	678	7,585
Tulsa	183,740	67,946	160,360	258,614	7,940	6,856	10,198	19,681
Utica	101,513	182,749	99,938	230,833	15,800	34,763	15,029	23,445
Wichita	168,279	54,011	171,208	172,023	9,626	7,327	10,416	32,905
Wilkes-Barre	76,826	315,415	95,607	251,365	12,025	23,583	12,795	30,959
Wilmington, Del.	110,358	158,029	95,827	270,330	15,823	22,006	23,944	35,505
Worcester	203,486	72,850	186,587	136,719	46,847	6,404	35,484	12,076
Youngstown	168,330	360,168	166,689	342,317	29,477	79,177	20,480	48,604

Retailing				Services				Wholesaling			
1948		1963		1948		1963		1948		1963	
City	Ring	City	Ring	City	Ring	City	Ring	City	Ring	City	Ring
10,691	4,660	6,683	34,297	3,264	1,681	2,893	14,643	4,285	1,731	2,847	12,184
63,262	60,927	40,963	63,416	19,362	10,992	54,491	28,407	66,265	8,452	59,373	27,405
30,496	8,418	28,148	17,118	9,182	2,394	12,839	3,902	15,777	3,622	18,997	4,371
19,632	17,955	13,130	25,358	5,577	4,612	6,008	7,003	8,091	3,004	8,146	5,910
9,000	3,986	6,676	6,520	2,656	777	2,646	1,162	2,466	740	2,419	1,032
22,191	1,028	20,885	5,875	5,976	1,906	8,979	1,778	10,982	274	12,342	1,347
25,002	4,355	22,855	18,963	8,332	1,787	9,661	2,954	8,223	408	9,244	2,747
12,127	2,052	9,885	25,408	3,531	388	3,880	7,569	5,259	1,133	4,557	6,260
67,607	29,843	44,066	58,357	24,240	6,429	27,547	14,059	45,139	3,206	34,297	14,149
14,246	2,569	15,772	9,334	4,462	622	7,409	2,078	9,185	774	10,614	2,506
23,977	1,179	21,499	11,484	6,388	2,371	10,314	4,545	9,113	351	9,519	3,645
18,861	6,039	23,856	23,938	6,759	2,129	12,243	8,709	4,769	779	6,702	3,646
58,361	62,451	53,231	93,085	27,137	7,184	38,404	37,337	49,613	15,851	35,452	35,756
34,186	6,858	29,863	29,499	11,192	1,291	13,382	6,399	20,024	2,081	19,306	8,042
8,700	667	7,709	4,644	3,140	226	2,770	1,694	4,503	408	4,169	2,022
10,513	1,005	10,447	2,485	3,408	208	4,037	489	5,389	503	5,554	756
12,860	11,554	11,054	14,759	3,806	2,616	4,042	3,433	393	105	371	301
18,107	3,405	14,380	13,808	5,530	508	6,454	3,045	7,603	535	7,892	4,250
8,614	1,890	8,943	4,501	2,614	446	2,106	888	3,167	172	3,648	411
10,074	11,964	7,704	33,824	3,935	4,281	3,868	13,148	5,582	2,530	5,271	10,560
22,390	3,224	17,390	12,301	6,511	361	7,134	2,684	8,182	839	8,308	3,214
9,139	3,136	7,192	7,637	3,064	780	3,339	2,716	2,044	674	2,500	1,274
5,873	1,352	2,786	11,987	1,509	252	1,207	5,512	1,045	144	564	2,374
13,402	1,430	8,887	11,430	4,752	289	4,245	4,344	6,080	492	4,680	4,758
6,696	5,955	5,509	8,998	2,271	1,167	2,111	2,112	2,470	663	2,386	1,101
12,923	1,219	9,931	8,762	4,800	311	4,122	3,004	5,699	549	4,516	3,041
7,028	9,957	4,492	8,679	1,734	2,230	1,638	1,753	2,421	2,136	1,826	2,796
9,867	3,566	8,234	13,514	2,839	634	3,878	2,011	3,547	899	5,117	2,172
13,700	2,569	11,427	4,792	2,708	1,160	3,606	932	4,420	225	4,940	660
12,684	13,586	9,615	12,159	3,583	2,395	3,313	2,348	3,679	1,243	3,689	2,307

Sources: Same as for table 9.

3

Population and Employment
Density Functions

The purpose of this chapter is to analyze in detail the process of suburbanization and decentralization in a sample of United States metropolitan areas. The subject was introduced in section 4 of chapter 2, which documented the broad outlines of postwar population and employment suburbanization in large United States metropolitan areas. The data analyzed there were census figures showing numbers and percentages of people living and working in central cities and suburban rings. Although such data can reveal the broad outlines of the massive postwar movement to the suburbs, they are subject to severe limitations.

First and most important, the central city–suburb dichotomy does not provide a fixed measure of suburbanization, since the part of the metropolitan area that is included in the central city differs greatly from one metropolitan area to another. The significance of a five point change in the percentage of residents living in the central city depends on whether the central city contains one-third or three-quarters of the area's residents. It is desirable to have a measure of suburbanization that does not depend on the historical accidents of central city boundary locations.

Second and closely related, some central city boundaries change through time, mainly because central cities annex parts of contiguous suburbs. Although corrections were made for boundary changes in the previous chapter, they are laborious and approximate at best. A measure of suburbanization is needed that does not depend on changing locations of central city boundaries.

Third, census data are highly aggregative across space (and, in the case of employment, across industries), providing only two observations on each variable for a given metropolitan area at a given point in time. It is possible, at some cost of time and effort, to obtain population data on a much less aggregative basis, since most population data are published for census tracts, of which there are several dozen in a large metropolitan area.

34

But employment is a different matter. Disclosure rules prevent the Census Bureau from publishing employment data on a more detailed basis than the city–suburb dichotomy except in a very few metropolitan areas. For some metropolitan areas it is possible to obtain detailed employment data either from local directories of manufacturers or from surveys made for local land use and transportation planning studies. And for some purposes these data have proved very useful to urban researchers. But the diversity of detail, coverage, definition, and timing among these sources makes it virtually impossible to obtain comparable and comprehensive data for a large number of metropolitan areas.

All three of the limitations described above can be surmounted if one knows or can assume something about the pattern of density in relation to distance from the city center. Indeed, several studies, to be surveyed in the next section, have provided strong evidence that population density falls off smoothly and at a decreasing rate as one moves out from the city center. These studies have found that the negative exponential density function provides a good approximation. It can be written

(1) $$D(u) = De^{-\gamma u}$$

where $D(u)$ is the density u miles from the center, e is the base of the natural logarithm, and D and γ are parameters to be estimated from the data. D is the measure of density at the city center and γ, which is positive, is a measure of the rate at which density declines with distance from the center. If γ is large, density falls off rapidly; if it is small, density falls off slowly.

The basic insight exploited in the present chapter is that, if (1) is an accurate representation of the density function, its estimation does not depend on where the central city boundary is drawn or on whether its location changes from time to time. Furthermore, since (1) is a two-parameter family of curves, it can be estimated with the two observations provided by the central city–suburb data.

If it is accepted that the exponential is the correct density function, central city–suburb data provide a perfectly acceptable way of estimating the density function. It must be emphasized that central city–suburb data are not merely a sample of two observations. They provide two exhaustive and exclusive integrals of the density function and thus make use of the entire population of data. There is no reason to believe that they provide less accurate estimates than would a large sample of census tract observations. But the dichotomous central city–suburb data cannot provide a test of goodness-of-fit of the exponential, or any two-parameter, function. The view taken here is that other studies have shown that the exponential function provides as good an approximation to urban population density data as any other function. The exponential function is therefore used here as part of the maintained hypothesis. The procedure makes it relatively easy to estimate density functions for times and places that would otherwise be practically impossible.

Employment density functions are, however, another matter. There is practically no evidence that the exponential density function provides an accurate description of the variation of employment density with distance from the city center. And the great concentration of employment in central business districts (CBDs) provides a prima facie case to the contrary. At best, the exponential function may provide a broad summary statistic to measure the concentration of employment near the centers of metropolitan areas. There are two justifications for proceeding boldly to calculate exponential employment density functions from central city–suburb data. First, there is no other way to do it, since more detailed data hardly exist. Second, exponential employment density functions provide extremely interesting comparisons between the suburbanization of population and that of employment. How much more suburbanized is population than employment? Has population suburbanized more than employment since World War II? The use of exponential employment density functions provides extremely simple answers to such questions. But the reader is warned that the price paid for such simplicity is an unknown loss of accuracy.

1. Previous Studies of Urban Density Functions

There have been many studies of suburbanization of population and employment in United States urban areas. A few recent studies are Kitagawa and Bogue [13], Moses and Williamson [25], and Niedercorn and Kain [29]. And there have been a few studies of urban density functions, which it is the purpose of this section to survey. But there have been no systematic comparisons among density functions for population and the various employment categories. Filling that gap is the major purpose of the present chapter.

The first extensive study of population density functions is that by Colin Clark [5]. Clark presents estimates of (1) for a large number of European, U.S., and Australian cities for a variety of years in the nineteenth and twentieth centuries, apparently using all data that were readily available. For each city, he drew a series of concentric rings, spaced at intervals of one mile, centered on the city center. Using census tract data, and excluding the central business districts, he calculated the average density at each concentric circle and regressed the natural log of density on distance from the city center. He concluded that density falls off exponentially in all cities at all times and that the density functions become flatter through time. The latter phenomenon is attributed to declining real cost of transportation through time.

Clark's study is deficient in several ways. He does not discuss the characteristics of his data, such as whether his densities are net or gross, how he handles bodies of water and other topographical irregularities, and how he identifies central business districts. His statistical procedure leaves something to be desired in that he presents no multiple correlation coefficients, significance tests of his regression coefficients, or tests for the linearity of his logarithmic regression equations. Finally, his statement that declining transportation costs cause density functions to flatten needs clarification and analysis. He apparently refers to the money costs of transportation. But opportunity cost of time spent traveling is a large part of commuting costs, and if opportunity cost rises with income, transportation cost may increase through time. Furthermore, the relationship between transportation cost and the density function is complex and Clark's statement of causality may or may not hold. This matter will be discussed again in later chapters. Nevertheless, Clark's historical generalization has been borne out by subsequent studies, and he was among the first to perceive the pattern.

By far the most careful and sophisticated estimation and analysis of urban population density functions is that of Richard Muth [26]. Muth selected for study the central cities of forty-six large urbanized areas, eliminating those with two or more central cities and those whose CBDs could not be identified. Within each of the forty-six central cities he selected twenty-five census tracts at random, and determined their gross population densities for 1950 and the distances from the center of the CBD to the centers of the census tracts.

For each city, Muth regressed the natural log of census tract population density on distance from the CBD center. The correlation coefficient between log of density and distance is significant for forty of the forty-six cities, and the median of the squared correlation coefficients is nearly one-half. A quadratic term in distance proved significant at the 10 percent level in twelve of the forty-six cities.

Muth's estimated density gradients vary from 0.07 to 1.20, but most fall between 0.20 and 0.50. He believed that differences in density gradients among metropolitan areas were to be explained by three sets of factors: the nature and cost of commuting transportation available to CBD workers; the spatial distribution of employment and shopping centers; and preferences for housing in various parts of the city.

He estimated and tested the importance of these factors by regressing the density gradients on several variables believed to be measures of the three sets of factors. Among the variables found to be significant in explaining the density gradients were car registrations per capita, the proportion of the metropolitan area's manufacturing employment located in the central city, the proportion of the area's urbanized population living in the central city, and the proportion of the central city's population that is Negro. Using these and similar variables, Muth was able to explain about 70 percent of the variance of the log of the density gradients.

Opinions of course differ as to what variables it is appropriate to use to explain urban population density. A major deficiency of many studies of urban land use and land value is that many explanatory variables in these studies are really endogenous to the urban economy. The basic problem is of course that whether a variable is endogenous or predetermined depends on the details of a simultaneous equation system, and few urban economists are accustomed to thinking in terms of simultaneous equation systems. Here, as elsewhere, Muth is ahead of most researchers. He tests whether some variables are exogenous by comparing his single equation estimates with simultaneous equation estimates. Since there is some overlap between Muth's sample and that analyzed later in this chapter, a comparison of the results is presented in the appendix to this chapter.

In an earlier study [20], the author formulated a small simultaneous equation model of land values and land uses in a metropolitan area. That model implied that the negative exponential function can be used to approximate the decline of both land values and the density of land uses as one moves out from the city center. The study presented a detailed analysis of land values and land uses in the Chicago metropolitan area. The measure of density was floor space per acre of land in several use categories: residential, manufacturing, commercial, and public. Regression of log of density on distance from the city center provided a good fit, but with uniformly lower R^2 than the regression of log of density on log of distance.

2. ESTIMATION PROCEDURE

The purpose of this section is to describe in detail how central city–suburb data can be used to estimate the negative exponential density function (1).

Suppose that (1) accurately represents the density of population or a certain employment category in a metropolitan area. Suppose further that the metropolitan area is circular in shape except that a pie slice of $2\pi - \phi$ radians has been taken out. (For Chicago, for example, ϕ is about equal to π. Extremely irregular metropolitan areas, such as San Francisco, probably cannot be approximated by this model.) Then the number of people

$n(u)$ in the category within a ring of width du, centered u miles from the city center, is

$$n(u)du = D(u)\phi u du,$$

and the total number of people in the category within k miles of the city center, $N(k)$, is

$$N(k) = \int_o^k n(u)du.$$

Substituting and integrating by parts, we get

(2) $$N(k) = \frac{\phi D}{\gamma^2} [1 - (1 + \gamma k)e^{-\gamma k}].$$

Letting k go to infinity, we get the total number of people in the category in question in the entire metropolitan area, N, where

(3) $$N = \frac{\phi D}{\gamma^2}.$$

Let k be the radius of the metropolitan area's central city; k was estimated by drawing on a map a semicircle whose center was at the city's center and whose boundary approximated as closely as possible the city's boundary. Cities with extremely irregular boundaries were excluded from the sample. The radius of the semicircle is then k. The estimate of ϕ was the value that would equate the area of a semicircular city of radius k to the area that the census gave for the city in question.

The numbers of people in the appropriate category in the central city and in the entire metropolitan area are obtained from census data. These numbers are the left hand sides of (2) and (3). The above procedure provides estimates of all the terms appearing in (2) and (3) except γ and D. Hence all that remains is to solve (1) and (3) simultaneously for γ and D. To do this, substitute N for the term outside the square brackets in (2). Then γ is the only unknown in (2). It was estimated iteratively by the Newton-Raphson method (see Scarborough [32]). When γ is thus calculated, it is substituted into (3), from which D is then calculated.

As was pointed out above, the procedure assumes that the urban population or employment density goes to zero as u goes to infinity. It is obviously not true, since metropolitan areas end a finite distance from the center and rural population and employment densities are finite. In fact, even rural densities decrease with distance from the SMSA center around many metropolitan areas. It can be shown that the assumption imparts a downward bias to estimates of γ, i.e., the estimated densities fall off too rapidly. Although I cannot prove it, I believe the bias is small. In any case, the main interest in density functions is to permit comparisons across space and time, and there is no reason to think they are affected by the biased estimates of γ.

3. POSTWAR POPULATION AND EMPLOYMENT DENSITY FUNCTIONS

In this section, estimates of (1) are presented and analyzed for population and several employment categories for a sample of United States metropolitan areas. The employment categories are those for which census data are widely available and for which suburbanization measures were presented in the previous chapter. Employment data pertain to the place of employment, whereas population data pertain to the place of residence.

The sample of metropolitan areas was chosen purposively rather than randomly. First, the shape of the central city and urbanized area had to be reasonably similar to semicircles. Although areas were not excluded just because political boundaries were irregular, they were excluded because of major topographical irregularities. San Francisco is an example of such

Table 11. Density Functions for Eighteen U.S. Metropolitan Areas

Metropolitan area		Population				Manufacturing			
		1948	1954	1958	1963	1948	1954	1958	1963
Albuquerque	γ	.56	.61	.61	.62	.71	.32	.49	.61
	D	5,748	11,387	14,148	18,180	157	151	253	483
Baltimore	γ	.48	.40	.36	.33	.48	.42	.37	.35
	D	51,159	42,693	37,481	34,541	6,815	5,575	4,665	4,059
Boston	γ	.27	.25	.23	.21	.29	.27	.25	.23
	D	35,473	32,629	28,630	24,922	4,853	4,336	3,788	3,292
Canton	γ	.69	.62	.58	.54	.94	.84	.80	.70
	D	19,994	18,724	17,610	16,591	7,814	6,374	5,143	4,130
Columbus	γ	.78	.65	.58	.52	.77	.76	.69	.63
	D	44,303	38,680	34,643	31,710	5,178	6,705	5,170	5,069
Denver	γ	.59	.45	.38	.33	.85	.64	.46	.36
	D	27,779	22,884	19,678	18,008	3,938	2,658	1,754	1,434
Houston	γ	.37	.28	.24	.21	.34	.30	.27	.23
	D	15,156	13,118	11,881	11,243	1,078	1,114	1,036	914
Milwaukee	γ	.47	.37	.32	.27	.48	.40	.35	.29
	D	58,318	44,262	37,823	31,123	12,996	8,954	7,048	5,189
Philadelphia	γ	.31	.27	.25	.23	.33	.30	.29	.26
	D	53,264	45,714	41,868	38,268	9,229	7,836	6,896	5,765
Phoenix	γ	.51	.39	.33	.28	.60	.52	.38	.31
	D	11,324	11,244	10,350	9,521	427	676	594	627
Pittsburgh	γ	.27	.25	.24	.22	.23	.22	.22	.26
	D	25,072	22,780	21,699	18,974	2,846	2,337	2,079	2,928
Rochester	γ	.73	.55	.47	.40	1.41	1.34	1.27	.89
	D	39,682	28,194	24,033	20,527	33,223	31,831	25,895	15,297
Sacramento	γ	.77	.56	.48	.41	1.03	.73	.44	.27
	D	22,120	18,337	16,782	15,262	1,405	925	634	409
San Antonio	γ	.63	.56	.50	.45	.97	.80	.48	.49
	D	27,513	28,705	25,855	23,951	2,293	1,823	732	902
San Diego	γ	.27	.23	.21	.20	.48	.36	.32	.30
	D	10,438	12,583	13,164	14,972	1,524	1,969	2,310	1,727
Toledo	γ	.83	.72	.67	.61	.98	.93	.85	.70
	D	41,123	34,661	31,768	28,151	10,638	8,414	6,223	5,517
Tulsa	γ	.89	.63	.50	.40	.62	.44	.43	.42
	D	28,788	20,126	15,339	11,947	905	890	892	839
Wichita	γ	.98	.74	.63	.54	.67	.37	.31	.33
	D	29,149	23,589	20,153	17,613	1,211	1,159	797	751

an exclusion. More important, semicircular shape is precluded if two or more large cities are too close to each other. The New York–Northeastern New Jersey, Chicago–Gary, and Los Angeles–Long Beach areas were excluded for this reason. Second, an attempt was made to include within the sample metropolitan areas with a large range of sizes. Third, an attempt was made to choose areas from different regions of the country. Fourth, areas with a wide range of historical growth rates were chosen. Finally, cities were chosen without any knowledge of their historical patterns of density changes. And all the calculations that were undertaken are reported here.

The sample consists of the eighteen SMSAs listed in table 11. Density functions were calculated for population and each of four employment categories (manufacturing, retailing, services, and wholesaling) for 1948, 1954, 1958, and 1963. (Population data were interpolated between census years to correspond to years for which employment data were available.) In total, we have the 360 density functions (18 × 5 × 4) shown in table 11.

Retailing				Services				Wholesaling			
)48	1954	1958	1963	1948	1954	1958	1963	1948	1954	1958	1963
.26	1.16	.91	.77	1.49	1.20	.93	.80	1.02	1.14	.88	.72
691	1,971	1,611	1,376	757	742	618	542	355	700	520	450
.72	.60	.50	.40	.76	.67	.62	.48	.91	.87	.76	.63
029	5,086	4,073	2,587	2,300	1,955	2,326	1,400	3,974	3,555	2,878	2,188
.38	.37	.33	.28	.44	.43	.44	.39	.57	.52	.46	.38
500	4,315	3,622	2,564	1,758	1,771	2,193	1,980	4,390	3,537	2,807	1,986
.94	.91	.86	.71	1.20	1.05	.95	.89	1.26	1.25	1.08	.98
146	1,965	1,848	1,256	817	647	599	538	908	1,030	752	722
.08	.90	.78	.53	1.42	1.00	.80	.64	1.03	.84	.77	.63
017	4,601	3,516	1,849	3,287	1,809	1,254	1,064	1,881	1,394	1,253	967
.83	.65	.52	.39	1.12	.77	.61	.52	1.25	.89	.75	.62
876	2,617	2,094	1,366	2,203	1,272	1,112	1,019	4,886	2,315	2,007	1,561
.46	.41	.33	.27	.55	.45	.36	.30	.58	.50	.39	.32
593	1,431	1,069	778	755	642	558	485	1,267	1,129	824	635
.63	.53	.46	.30	.72	.57	.54	.37	.75	.59	.49	.36
951	4,666	3,857	1,877	2,443	1,758	1,955	1,001	4,042	2,528	1,947	1,035
.37	.44	.30	.26	.43	.42	.39	.36	.59	.49	.44	.37
182	5,797	2,855	2,889	1,604	1,685	1,720	1,710	4,139	3,058	2,529	1,891
.04	.69	.44	.31	.97	.71	.45	.31	1.07	.71	.46	.34
643	1,477	909	627	741	567	396	268	1,096	726	404	277
.41	.37	.35	.33	.52	.53	.49	.50	.74	.68	.62	.50
323	2,260	2,142	1,809	1,306	1,435	1,334	1,437	3,284	1,820	1,510	1,495
.00	1.12	.90	.54	.93	1.24	1.05	.82	1.42	1.39	1.22	.84
672	5,519	3,811	1,941	1,393	2,413	1,967	1,350	2,770	2,955	2,434	1,338
.47	1.09	.72	.45	1.47	1.19	.83	.48	1.36	1.07	.89	.61
876	3,227	1,868	1,137	1,368	1,240	819	500	1,882	1,080	863	662
.03	.75	.60	.47	.55	.76	.59	.51	1.08	.83	.62	.54
248	2,614	1,805	1,160	422	1,006	737	615	1,757	1,178	720	611
.34	.29	.26	.21	.35	.31	.30	.25	.43	.33	.30	.28
916	859	877	671	347	345	480	417	327	245	276	258
.03	1.03	.80	.56	1.34	1.18	.96	.74	1.14	1.11	.95	.73
325	3,894	2,396	1,482	1,964	1,765	1,252	856	1,866	1,714	1,367	977
.35	.97	.68	.51	1.57	1.01	.72	.57	1.46	1.03	.75	.57
302	2,363	1,459	841	1,978	1,065	656	444	2,230	1,160	777	488
.42	1.13	.83	.62	1.58	1.09	.89	.68	1.42	1.15	.84	.70
538	3,506	1,975	1,144	2,031	1,005	683	524	2,005	1,318	821	589

The calculated density functions display a remarkably consistent pattern of flattening through time. There are only fifteen cases in which a gradient becomes steeper between successive years for which it was calculated. Of the fifteen increases, four are by only .01. Five are in Albuquerque, three in Pittsburgh, two each in Rochester and San Antonio, and one each in Boston, Philadelphia, and Wichita. By sector, there are five increases each in manufacturing and services, two each in population and retailing, and one in wholesaling.

It is reasonable to say that the larger is γ the more centralized or less suburbanized is the sector. Unweighted averages of γ for the five sectors and the four years are shown in table 12. By this measure, population is the least centralized, or most suburbanized, sector, followed by manufacturing, retailing, services, and wholesaling in that order. Furthermore, although all sectors have suburbanized, their ranking by degree of suburbanization has remained unchanged during the fifteen-year period. Table 12 also shows that the degree of suburbanization has become more uniform among the sectors during the postwar period. The difference between the largest and smallest of the averages of γ was smaller both absolutely and relatively in 1963 than in 1948. In 1948, the largest average γ was almost one and three-fourths times the smallest, whereas in 1963 it was just less than one and one-half times the smallest.

The tendency toward convergence among the gradients for different sectors has not been documented in earlier studies. Presumably, there will be more commuting the greater the divergence between the gradients for population and the employment sectors. This matter will be explored further in later chapters.

The parameters vary a great deal from SMSA to SMSA. For population, D varies by a factor of 10, from just less than 6,000 to about 60,000. There is an obvious and expected tendency for D to be large in large metropolitan areas; γ varies much less. Again taking population as an example, it ranges from a low of 0.2 to a high of nearly 1.0. There appears to be some tendency for cities that are large and that have had rapid recent growth to have small γ's. There are, however, many exceptions to these tendencies, and a detailed analysis of the determinants of density function parameters is presented in section 5.

Table 12. Averages of Gradients by Sector and Year, Eighteen Metropolitan Areas

Sector	1948	1954	1958	1963
Population	.58	.47	.42	.38
Manufacturing	.68	.55	.48	.42
Retailing	.88	.75	.59	.44
Services	.97	.81	.66	.53
Wholesaling	1.00	.86	.70	.56

D is clearly much more strongly affected by SMSA size than is γ. Within a particular sector and SMSA, D does not vary much more, in proportion to its magnitude, than does γ. In the employment sectors, D and γ may be affected by systematic departures of density from the exponential form. For example, the growth of suburban employment centers might affect the estimated D even if $D(o)$ were unchanged, and the estimated γ even if the density gradient were unchanged throughout the rest of the SMSA.

All the data analyzed so far pertain to the period following World War II. The striking pattern of flattening density functions in almost all SMSAs and sectors raises the question whether this is a continuation of a prewar pattern or whether there has been a break in the historical pattern. Much popular literature is written as though suburbanization were mainly a postwar phenomenon, induced by the circumstances of urban life peculiar to the period. For example, it is sometimes claimed that home mortgage insurance by the federal government has been mainly responsible for postwar suburbanization. Or, it is claimed, postwar suburbanization has resulted mainly from the attempt of whites to flee from the increasing numbers of blacks in central cities. Finally, postwar suburbanization is sometimes attributed to the rapid growth of automobile ownership during the period. All three of these factors have operated somewhat otherwise during the postwar period than during earlier times. If they are the major factors responsible, we should expect postwar suburbanization to have been faster than prewar.

Of course, the answer one gets depends on the measure of suburbanization one uses. Frequently, the measure used is the growth of population and employment in suburbs in relation to that in central cities. But by that measure suburbanization is an almost inevitable result of growth since, under any reasonable set of assumptions, the number and proportion of people living and working beyond the edge of the central city will grow as the metropolitan area's population and employment grow (unless the city's boundaries are moved out as the area grows). A better way to test the hypothesis that different forces have been at work in the postwar period is to see whether the pattern of shifting density functions has been different from that in the prewar period. If special forces have been at work in the postwar period, the rate of flattening of density functions should be greater than in the prewar period.

4. Prewar Density Functions

Available U.S. census data make it possible to estimate some density functions as far back as the nineteenth century. Between 1920 and 1940, the census used an urban concept called a metropolitan district. A metro-

politan district consisted of a central city and any contiguous minor civil
divisions (towns, boroughs, etc.) that met a certain population density
criterion. It is not possible to adjust these data for boundary changes, but
it was shown in section 2 that the method employed provides estimates of
density functions that do not depend on the location of central city boundaries. Between 1880 and 1920, population data are available for cities
and minor civil subdivisions, but they are not grouped into metropolitan
areas. The problems of estimating density functions are therefore much
greater and the estimates are correspondingly less reliable. Therefore, data
are first presented for a sample of density functions between 1920 and
1940. These will be followed by a small sample of estimates for ten-year
intervals between 1880 and 1920.

The farther back one goes, the fewer the metropolitan areas and sectors for which data are available. Furthermore, at any point in time, most
data are collected for relatively large metropolitan areas. Thus, the need
to restrict the sample to metropolitan areas that not only are large now
but also have been large for some time inevitably biases the sample toward
slowly growing areas. It was decided to select six of the metropolitan areas
studied in section 3 and to estimate density functions back to 1920 for as
many sectors as possible. The major criterion for selection of metropolitan
areas was data availability, but an effort was made to select areas with a
variety of sizes and geographical locations. Much of the available data per-
tains to metropolitan areas in the northeastern part of the country. All the
data are from censuses of populations, manufactures, and business.

Density functions for the six cities are presented in table 13. For convenience of reference, the postwar density functions for the six cities are
repeated from table 11. The obvious implication of the estimates in table
13 is that the process of flattening of density functions started long before
World War II. The relative frequency of increases in density gradients is
about as great in table 13 as it was in table 11.

To facilitate comparison with the data in table 12, average density
gradients by sector and year are presented for the six metropolitan areas in
table 14. The last four columns of table 14 show the six-area averages for
the years and sectors for which table 12 shows eighteen-area averages.
Comparison between corresponding entries shows that the six metropolitan
areas are by no means entirely representative of the eighteen areas.

For the population sector, the average of the six gradients fell by an
average of .012 points per year during the forty-three-year period. The
period of slowest suburbanization was the 1930s, when the average gradient fell by .007 points per year. The fastest suburbanization occurred
between 1948 and 1954, when the average gradient fell by .018 points per
year, more than twice as fast as during the 1930s. Between 1940 and 1948,

Table 13. Density Functions for Six U.S. Metropolitan Areas

Metropolitan area		1920	1930	1940	1948	1954	1958	1963
				Population				
Baltimore	γ	.70	.64	.60	.48	.40	.36	.33
	D	69,238	67,630	65,542	51,159	42,693	37,481	34,541
Denver	γ	.87	.83	.76	.59	.45	.38	.33
	D	34,870	36,265	35,334	27,779	22,884	19,678	18,008
Milwaukee	γ	.61	.56	.51	.47	.37	.32	.27
	D	68,304	74,209	65,434	58,318	44,262	37,823	31,123
Philadelphia	γ	.25	.37	.36	.31	.27	.25	.23
	D	67,595	62,034	59,789	53,264	45,714	41,868	38,268
Rochester	γ	1.18	.96	.88	.73	.55	.47	.40
	D	72,729	58,464	50,775	39,682	28,194	24,033	20,527
Toledo	γ	1.43	1.01	.93	.83	.72	.67	.61
	D	85,828	56,260	47,031	41,123	34,661	31,768	28,151
				Manufacturing				
Baltimore	γ	.70	.66	.49	.48	.42	.37	.35
	D	9,478	7,547	4,416	6,815	5,575	4,665	4,059
Denver	γ	1.07	.94	.92	.85	.64	.46	.36
	D	3,215	2,506	1,710	3,938	2,658	1,754	1,434
Milwaukee	γ	.52	.44	.40	.48	.40	.35	.29
	D	11,713	8,921	5,012	12,996	8,954	7,048	5,189
Philadelphia	γ	.32	.35	.32	.33	.30	.29	.26
	D	7,586	7,332	5,243	9,229	7,836	6,896	5,765
Rochester	γ	1.51	1.28	1.32	1.41	1.34	1.27	.89
	D	24,514	16,493	14,235	33,223	31,831	25,895	15,297
Toledo	γ	1.55	1.24	1.16	.98	.93	.85	.70
	D	17,097	13,214	6,570	10,638	8,414	6,223	5,517

Metropolitan area		1929	1939	1948	1954	1958	1963
			Retailing				
Baltimore	γ	1.02	.88	.72	.60	.50	.40
	D	7,257	6,592	7,029	5,086	4,073	2,587
Denver	γ	1.10	1.00	.83	.67	.52	.39
	D	3,933	3,697	3,876	2,617	2,094	1,366
Milwaukee	γ	.59	.56	.63	.53	.46	.30
	D	4,039	4,074	6,951	4,666	3,857	1,877
Philadelphia	γ	.47	.39	.37	.44	.30	.26
	D	4,493	3,118	4,182	5,797	2,855	2,229
Rochester	γ	1.35	1.24	1.00	1.12	.90	.54
	D	5,685	5,135	4,672	5,519	3,811	1,941
Toledo	γ	1.61	1.30	1.03	1.03	.80	.56
	D	6,501	4,486	4,325	3,894	2,396	1,482
			Services				
Baltimore	γ	1.07	.76	.67	.62	.48	
	D	2,777	2,300	1,955	2,326	1,400	
Denver	γ	1.24	1.12	.77	.61	.52	
	D	1,494	2,203	1,272	1,112	1,019	
Milwaukee	γ	.68	.72	.57	.54	.37	
	D	1,323	2,443	1,758	1,955	1,001	

Table 13 (continued)

Metropolitan area		1929	1939	1948	1954	1958	1963
		Services (continued)					
Philadelphia	γ		.49	.43	.42	.39	.36
	D		1,243	1,604	1,685	1,720	1,710
Rochester	γ		1.47	.93	1.24	1.05	.82
	D		1,144	1,393	2,413	1,967	1,350
Toledo	γ		1.76	1.34	1.18	.96	.74
	D		1,660	1,964	1,765	1,252	856
		Wholesaling					
Baltimore	γ	1.54	1.49	.91	.87	.76	.63
	D	7,639	6,866	3,974	3,555	2,878	2,188
Denver	γ	1.61	1.51	1.25	.89	.75	.62
	D	4,393	3,645	4,856	2,315	2,007	1,561
Milwaukee	γ	.78	.77	.75	.59	.49	.36
	D	3,045	2,609	4,042	2,528	1,947	1,035
Philadelphia	γ	.70	.63	.59	.49	.44	.37
	D	4,384	2,934	4,139	3,058	2,529	1,891
Rochester	γ	1.63	1.40	1.42	1.39	1.22	.84
	D	2,697	1,732	2,770	2,955	2,434	1,338
Toledo	γ	2.29	1.63	1.14	1.11	.95	.73
	D	6,393	2,405	1,866	1,714	1,367	977

the average gradient fell by .0125 per year. The rate of flattening was about the same between 1920 and 1930 as between 1958 and 1963, about .01 points per year. All these findings are in accord with intuitive expectations. Suburbanization proceeded rather quickly during the prosperous 1920s, when the use of automobiles for commuting increased rapidly. It proceeded slowly during the depression of the 1930s, and very rapidly during the prosperous war and postwar years after 1940. It is, however, notable that there is evidence of deceleration in the suburbanization process during the latest period. Deceleration was also evident in table 12, based on the larger sample of eighteen metropolitan areas.

It is clear from table 14 that the employment sectors were suburbanizing steadily before World War II. The prewar data in table 14 show the same ranking of sectors by degree of suburbanization that table 12 shows

Table 14. Averages of Gradients by Sector and Year, Six Metropolitan Areas

Sector	1920	1929	1939	1948	1954	1958	1963
Population*	.84	.73	.67	.57	.46	.41	.36
Manufacturing	.95	.82	.77	.76	.67	.60	.48
Retailing	n.a.	1.02	.90	.76	.73	.58	.41
Services	n.a.	n.a.	1.12	.88	.81	.70	.55
Wholesaling	n.a.	1.43	1.24	1.01	.89	.77	.59

* Figures in columns headed 1929 and 1939 are for 1930 and 1940 respectively.
n.a. = not available.

for the postwar period. However, the postwar ranking is slightly different for the six areas in table 14 from that for the eighteen areas in table 12. Table 14 also shows the convergence among the gradients that was observed in table 12. The largest entry in table 14 for 1929 is almost twice as large as the smallest (assuming that the unavailable average for services is less than the average for wholesaling; otherwise, the convergence is even greater), whereas the largest entry for 1963 is less than two-thirds larger than the smallest. It is interesting to observe the behavior of the difference between the average gradients for population and manufacturing. In the prewar period, the average gradient for population was about 0.1 less than that for manufacturing. The difference widened to about 0.2 in the early postwar years of rapid population suburbanization. But by 1963, rapid suburbanization of manufacturing had narrowed the difference to little more than its prewar value. This finding suggests strongly that the movement of people to the suburbs has attracted manufacturing employment to the suburbs rather than vice versa.

The data in table 14 suggest strongly that rapid suburbanization in the early postwar years was the result of catching up after the stagnation of the 1930s rather than of important new forces. During the 1920s, both population and manufacturing employment suburbanized at about their average rates for the forty-four-year period. Suburbanization decelerated drastically during the 1930s, and then proceeded rapidly after the war· By the early 1960s, suburbanization of population had decelerated, but the employment sectors were still suburbanizing rapidly. This analysis leads to the anticipation that suburbanization of population may have continued to decelerate during the latter 1960s and that deceleration may have begun in the employment sectors.

This section will be concluded with a small sample of data going back to 1880. Before 1920, the census published population data for central cities and for minor civil divisions. No usable data are available for employment. It was necessary to put the population data together by meaningful metropolitan areas. This was done with the aid of Bartholomew [3], a study that shows the locations of minor civil divisions. Areas were measured with a planimeter, and population densities were computed for all minor civil divisions near the central city. The metropolitan area was designated to be the central city and all surrounding minor civil divisions with population density of at least 125 people per square mile. This is the density criterion that was used by the census to designate metropolitan districts between 1920 and 1940. The procedure yielded population and area for central cities, and population for the suburban ring. From this point on, the computational procedure is the same as that employed previously.

The intention was to apply the procedure to all six metropolitan

areas for census years between 1880 and 1910. However, not enough minor
civil divisions around Toledo had the requisite density to compute suburban population, and Denver was so small that the census did not present
data. It was thus possible to compute density functions for only four of the
six metropolitan areas. The computed density functions, along with those
for the more recent years from table 13, are presented in table 15.

Despite the complex and somewhat subjective way the estimates were
made for years before 1920, the density functions appear to be consistent
with those for more recent years except in the case of Philadelphia. Philadelphia was by far the hardest metropolitan area to work with, since more
than 100 minor civil divisions were involved and their boundaries and
names changed frequently. It is likely that the recorded increase in Philadelphia's density gradient between 1920 and 1930 is illusory rather than
real and that the estimated gradients for earlier years are too low. Otherwise, we again see the previously recorded trend of steadily decreasing
density gradients.

Table 16 shows the average population density gradients for the four
metropolitan areas for the period 1880–1963. The data provide a remarkable statistical picture of the massive suburbanization of U.S. metropolitan
areas. During the eighty-three-year period, the average density gradient
of the four metropolitan areas fell by three-fourths of its 1880 value. The

Table 15. Population Density Functions for Four U.S. Metropolitan Areas

Year	Baltimore	Milwaukee	Philadelphia	Rochester
1880 γ	1.82	.97	.30	1.78
D	244,730	44,287	39,948	51,400
1890 γ	1.08	.92	.28	1.83
D	89,300	70,804	45,555	81,600
1900 γ	1.05	.90	.28	1.59
D	101,200	92,374	56,611	74,500
1910 γ	0.93	.78	.28	1.20
D	90,100	77,764	64,772	58,400
1920 γ	.70	.61	.25	1.18
D	69,238	68,304	67,595	72,729
1930 γ	.64	.56	.37	.96
D	67,630	74,209	62,034	58,464
1940 γ	.60	.51	.36	.88
D	65,542	65,434	59,787	50,775
1948 γ	.48	.47	.31	.73
D	51,159	58,318	53,264	39,682
1954 γ	.40	.37	.27	.55
D	42,693	44,262	45,714	28,194
1958 γ	.36	.32	.25	.47
D	37,481	37,823	41,868	24,033
1963 γ	.33	.27	.23	.40
D	34,541	31,123	38,268	20,527

Table 16. Averages of Gradients for Population-Density Functions, Four Metropolitan Areas

Year	Average gradient	Year	Average gradient
1880	1.22	1940	.59
1890	1.06	1948	.50
1900	.96	1954	.40
1910	.80	1958	.35
1920	.69	1963	.31
1930	.63		

dramatic nature of this shift can be portrayed in another way. Consider a metropolitan area whose density gradient equals the average for the four areas. In 1880, half the people in this representative metropolitan area lived within 1.3 miles of the city center. In 1963, half the people lived within 5.5 miles of the city center.[1]

Considering the nature of the data, there is surprisingly little variability from one period to another in the rate at which the metropolitan areas decentralized. There is no evidence at all that the rate of decentralization is more rapid in recent than in earlier years. The average annual decrease in the average gradient during periods between estimates is as follows:

1880–90	1890–1900	1900–10	1910–20	1920–30
.016	.010	.016	.017	.006

1930–40	1940–48	1948–54	1954–58	1958–63
.004	.011	.017	.012	.008

The average for the entire period is 0.11. In this small sample, the most rapid suburbanization occurred between 1910 and 1920 and between 1948 and 1954. But suburbanization was almost as fast between 1880 and 1890 and between 1900 and 1910. The slowest suburbanization occurred between 1930 and 1940, not surprisingly. And the most recent period, 1958–63, is below the average for the entire period.

Although the subject of the chapter is suburbanization, it is useful to conclude this section of the chapter with a reminder that suburbanization takes place within a context of metropolitan area growth. Table 17 shows the population growth of the four metropolitan areas during the eighty-three-year period. In 1963, the four metropolitan areas had five times their 1880 population. (The 1963 population of the United States was less

1. It is a property of the exponential function that the fraction of people living within any distance of the center depends only on γ and not on D, ϕ, or N. The fraction living within k miles of the center is the ratio of (2) to (3) above.

Table 17. Population of Four Metropolitan Areas, 1880, 1930, 1963

(*in thousands*)

Metropolitan area	1880	1930	1963
Baltimore	366	949	1,823
Milwaukee	130	743	1,341
Philadelphia	1,031	2,847	4,344
Rochester	102	399	733
Total	1,629	4,938	8,241

than four times its 1880 population.) The smallest of the four metropolitan areas, Rochester and Milwaukee, had the most rapid growth, and the largest, Philadelphia, had the slowest growth. But the four areas did not change their ranks during the eighty-three-year period.

5. Determinants of Density Functions

The relationship between intensity of land use for any purpose and distance from the center of a metropolitan area is complex and can be explored adequately only within the framework of a detailed model of urban structure. Most theoretical models of urban structure suggest that the negative exponential density function is at best a rough approximation to reality and that any exogenous change is likely to affect land use intensity in complex ways.

The justification for the use of the negative exponential density function in this and other studies is its computational convenience, its approximate accuracy at certain levels of aggregation, and its value as an easily understood descriptive summary. But since the negative exponential-density function is not closely related to detailed theoretical models, attempts to specify the determinants of its parameters are somewhat intuitive and unrigorous. The major problems are to decide which variables should be taken to be exogenous determinants of the density function parameters, the direction of the effect, and the form of the relationship. Ideally, all these questions should be answered with the help of a general equilibrium model. Nevertheless, it is possible to overstress this point. Many empirical studies in economics are less closely related to theoretical models than would be ideal. Most empirical studies of consumer demand, for example, are not much more closely related to the theory of consumer demand than density function studies are to theories of urban structure.

Changes in urban density functions involve the erection, alteration, and demolition of structures, which have notoriously long lives. It is therefore important to distinguish carefully between the determinants of equilibrium values of parameters of density functions and the process of adjustment from one equilibrium value to another. In view of the widespread recognition that structures have very long lives, it is surprising that studies of density functions have paid no attention to the disequilibrium adjustment process.

It is assumed here that the equilibrium values of the parameters of the density functions are determined as follows:

a. Size of SMSA. It seems clear that in equilibrium D should be an increasing function of the size of the SMSA. Almost any conceivable model would imply that large metropolitan areas would extend farther both upward and outward than small ones. γ should be a decreasing function of SMSA size, since large SMSAs can support subcenters for shopping and employment and are therefore less dependent on the city center than are small SMSAs. The most obvious measure of size is the SMSA population. For the employment categories, however, total SMSA employment in the category may also be a determinant of D and γ.

b. Income. There is a high income elasticity of demand for high-quality, low-density housing. It follows that in the residential sector both D and γ should be decreasing functions of family income in equilibrium. There does not, however, appear to be any reason to believe that family income should directly affect the density functions in the employment categories. There may of course be an indirect effect in that suburbanization of population may cause suburbanization of employment and vice versa. It would mean that the structural equation for the population γ should contain the employment γ and vice versa. That each sector's γ is omitted from the equations for other sectors' γ means that the equations are reduced-form, rather than structural, equations.

c. Transportation prices. A decrease in the relative price of transportation per passenger mile will presumably lead to an increase in passenger miles traveled. For given amounts and densities of land devoted to other purposes, the result will be an increase in land used as an input in the transportation sector. Thus, more land will be used by the SMSA, and population and employment will be spread more thinly over the larger amount of land. This argument implies that D and γ should be decreasing functions of transportation prices in equilibrium. The difficulty with the foregoing argument is that a change in the relative price of transportation does affect the amounts of nontransportation activities in the metropolitan area and the intensities of their land uses. Consequently it is difficult to predict the effect of transportation prices on density functions. A practical difficulty is that it is hard to get data on transportation prices. Real operating costs per passenger mile of transportation vehicles probably have fallen during the postwar period, but a large part of commuting cost is the opportunity cost of time spent traveling, which presumably rises with income. The temptation is to introduce time as a proxy for the price and technology of transportation in the explanation of variations in density function parameters. Although the tradition of using time as a proxy for the state of technology is well established in economics, just what the result means may be less clear in this application than in others. If time should be omitted, its inclusion is a specification error and may bias coefficient estimates.

There is little theoretical basis for choosing among alternative forms of the relationships between parameters of the density functions and the explanatory variables, but linear and log linear forms have been most successful in previous studies.

The foregoing suggests estimation of the following relationships:

$$(4) \qquad D_{it}^* = \alpha_o^* + \alpha_1^* P_{it} + \alpha_2^* Y_{it} + \alpha_3^* t + \eta_{it}$$

and

$$(5) \qquad \gamma_{it}^* = \beta_o^* + \beta_1^* P_{it} + \beta_2^* Y_{it} + \beta_3^* t + \epsilon_{it}$$

for the population sector, and

$$(6) \qquad D_{it}^* = \alpha_o^* + \alpha_1^* P_{it} + \alpha_2^* N_{it} + \alpha_3^* t + \eta_{it}$$

and

$$(7) \qquad \gamma_{it}^* = \beta_o^* + \beta_1^* P_{it} + \beta_2^* N_{it} + \beta_3^* t + \epsilon_{it}$$

separately for each employment category; and the logarithmic counterparts of these equations. In these equations, D_{it}^* and γ_{it}^* are the equilibrium values of D and γ in the ith SMSA and the tth time period. P stands for the population of the SMSA, Y for median family income, N for SMSA employment in the relevant category, and t for time (the unit interval being five years); η and ϵ are disturbance terms.

Starred values of γ and D represent equilibrium values and are unobserved except in the unlikely event the system is in equilibrium. It is assumed that the adjustment of γ and D to equilibrium can be approximated by the well-known distributed-lag adjustment process, which assumes that between successive observations the variable adjusts by a constant fraction of its deviation from equilibrium in the earlier period. This process can be represented by

$$(8) \qquad D_{it} - D_{it-1} = \mu(D_{it}^* - D_{it-1})$$

and

$$(9) \qquad \gamma_{it} - \gamma_{it-1} = \lambda(\gamma_{it}^* - \gamma_{it-1})$$

where μ and λ are the adjustment coefficients.

Substituting the right-hand sides of (4)–(7) for D^* and γ^* in (8) and (9) gives

(10) $\qquad D_{it} = \alpha_o + \alpha_1 P_{it} + \alpha_2 Y_{it} + \alpha_3 t + (1 - \mu)D_{it-1} + \eta_{it}$

and

(11) $\qquad \gamma_{it} = \beta_o + \beta_1 P_{it} + \beta_2 Y_{it} + \beta_3 t + (1 - \lambda)\gamma_{it-1} + \epsilon_{it}$

for the household sector, and

(12) $\qquad D_{it} = \alpha_o + \alpha_1 P_{it} + \alpha_2 N_{it} + \alpha_3 t + (1 - \mu)D_{it-1} + \eta_{it}$

and

(13) $\qquad \gamma_{it} = \beta_o + \beta_1 P_{it} + \beta_2 N_{it} + \beta_3 t + (1 - \lambda)\gamma_{it-1} + \epsilon_{it}$

for the employment sectors. In these equations, $\alpha_j = \mu \alpha_j^*$ and $\beta_j = \lambda \beta_j^*$. (The logarithmic analogs to (4)–(13) are obtained by writing the logarithms of the variables instead of the variables themselves. The logarithmic versions of (8) and (9) assume that D and γ change by a constant fraction of the percentage deviation from equilibrium each period, rather than by a constant fraction of the numerical deviation, as in (8) and (9).) All the variables in (10)–(13) are observable, and from estimates of (10)–(13) it is easy to derive estimates of the starred parameters and of λ and μ.

Estimates of (10)–(13) are presented in table 18; the derived estimates of (4)–(7) are in table 19. Estimates of the logarithmic analogs to (10)–(13) are in table 20; the derived estimates of the logarithmic analogs to (4)–(7) are in table 21. Sample points are D and γ shown in table 11.[2] Figures in parentheses below the coefficients are t-values.

R^2 in tables 18 and 20 is consistently large. None is below 0.65, and only those for retailing are below 0.70. R^2 in the equations for γ is not very different from that in the equations for D. Nor is R^2 for the logarithmic equations very different from that for the linear equations. (Of course, a different sum of squares is minimized in the logarithmic equations than in the linear equations.) Many of the t-statistics are disturbingly small, especially in the linear regressions. Only the lagged dependent variable is consistently highly significant. Some reassurance is provided by the consistency of the sign pattern of coefficients among the employment sectors other than manufacturing. But the regression equations in tables 18 and 20 do not quite rule out the possibility that the entire process of flattening of urban density functions is a first-order Markov process in which γ responds to a once-for-all change in its equilibrium values.

2. The prewar data in Table 13 could not be used because the interval between observations was longer than for the postwar data.

Table 18. Linear Regressions for Parameters of Density Functions

Dependent variable		Constant term	Population	SMSA median family income	SMSA sector employment	Time	Lagged dependent variable	R^2
Population	γ	$.1635(10)^{-1}$ (.3448)	$-.4453(10)^{-8}$ (−.5696)	$-.8827(10)^{-5}$ (−.8353)		$.2531(10)^{-1}$ (1.6307)	.7952 (18.5037)	.937
	D	$.3209(10)^4$ (1.8989)	$.6710(10)^{-3}$ (2.1342)	−.5439 (−1.0244)		$.8863(10)^{-3}$ (1.1193)	.7651 (28.4906)	.961
Manufacturing	γ	$-.2070(10)^{-1}$ (−.2848)	$-.7805(10)^{-7}$ (−1.3396)		$.6411(10)^{-6}$ (1.5059)	$.2038(10)^{-1}$ (1.2125)	.7997 (14.2689)	.874
	D	$.8525(10)^3$ (1.3189)	$.4850(10)^{-3}$ (.6320)		$-.3086(10)^{-2}$ (−.5130)	$-.3125(10)^{-3}$ (−1.5155)	.8123 (28.6586)	.960
Retailing	γ	.2063 (2.4802)	$.2797(10)^{-7}$ (.4106)		$-.5479(10)^{-6}$ (−.4000)	$-.4932(10)^{-1}$ (−3.1767)	.7225 (13.6722)	.906
	D	$.1015(10)^4$ (1.9254)	$-.4692(10)^{-3}$ (−.8103)		$.1135(10)^{-1}$ (.9647)	$-.2070(10)^{-3}$ (−1.5946)	.5598 (8.2627)	.692
Services	γ	.2310 (2.3179)	$.5840(10)^{-7}$ (.7959)		$-.3641(10)^{-5}$ (−.8708)	$-.3048(10)^{-1}$ (−1.5101)	.6607 (11.5080)	.856
	D	$.5342(10)^3$ (2.5511)	$-.5904(10)^{-4}$ (−.2798)		$.1438(10)^{-1}$ (1.1848)	$-.1308(10)^{-3}$ (−2.2839)	.5640 (8.2627)	.744
Wholesaling	γ	$.8749(10)^{-1}$ (−.9473)	$.5533(10)^{-7}$ (1.0653)		$-.2350(10)^{-5}$ (−.9426)	$-.2731(10)^{-1}$ (1.5915)	.8092 (14.8281)	.895
	D	$.2792(10)^3$ (1.2488)	$.7225(10)^{-4}$ (.4024)		$.1421(10)^{-2}$ (.1581)	$-.5938(10)^{-2}$ (−.9722)	.6337 (12.1947)	.877

Table 19. Linear Regressions for Parameters of Equilibrium-Density Functions

Dependent variable		Constant term	Population	SMSA median family income	SMSA sector employment	Time
Population	γ^*	$.7984(10)^{-1}$	$-.2174(10)^{-7}$	$-.4310(10)^{-4}$		.1236
	D^*	$.1366(10)^5$	$.2856(10)^{-6}$	$-.2315(10)^{-1}$		$.3773(10)^4$
Manufacturing	γ^*	−.1033	$-.3893(10)^{-6}$		$.3199(10)^{-6}$	.1017
	D^*	$.4692(10)^4$	$.2669(10)^{-6}$		$-.1699(10)^{-1}$	$-.1721(10)^4$
Retailing	γ^*	.7433	$.1008(10)^{-6}$		$-.1975(10)^{-6}$	−.1777
	D^*	$.2612(10)^4$	$-.1066(10)^{-2}$		$.2577(10)^{-1}$	$-.4703(10)^3$
Services	γ^*	.6809	$.1646(10)^{-6}$		$-.1073(10)^{-1}$	$-.8983(10)^{-1}$
	D^*	$.1225(10)^4$	$-.1354(10)^{-3}$		$-.3299(10)^{-1}$	$-.3000(10)^3$
Wholesaling	γ^*	.4585	$.2900(10)^{-6}$		$-.1232(10)^{-4}$	−.1431
	D^*	$.7621(10)^3$	$.1972(10)^{-3}$		$.3879(10)^{-2}$	$-.1621(10)^{-1}$

Table 20. Log Linear Regressions for Parameters of Density Functions

Dependent variable		Constant term	Log population	Log SMSA median family income	Log SMSA sector employment	Log time	Lagged dependent variable	R^2
Population	log γ	.9069 (.9806)	$-.2829(10)^{-1}$ (−1.2017)	−.1021 (−.9073)		.1415 (1.8125)	.9046 (19.8500)	.967
	log D	$.1756(10)^{1}$ (1.1508)	$.1679(10)^{-1}$ (.6691)	$.6223(10)^{-2}$ (.0323)		$-.4877(10)^{-1}$ (−.3634)	.7939 (20.0988)	.919
Manufacturing	log γ	−.1380 (−.2182)	$-.4706(10)^{-1}$ (−.6185)		$.3845(10)^{-1}$ (.7928)	.1020 (1.0838)	.8676 (12.4121)	.850
	log D	.8332 (1.1807)	$-.7051(10)^{-1}$ (−.7355)		.1034 (1.1985)	$-.6320(10)^{-1}$ (−.5330)	.8621 (20.5795)	.959
Retailing	log γ	−.1460 (−.1893)	$.7614(10)^{-1}$ (.4579)		$-.8330(10)^{-1}$ (−.5464)	−.2608 (−4.2090)	.8672 (12.4597)	.937
	log D	3.4309 (1.7690)	−.4434 (−.9936)		−.5069 (1.1295)	−.3362 (−1.8762)	.6519 (6.6274)	.653
Services	log γ	$-.1539(10)^{1}$ (−2.1154)	.9936 (2.4304)		−.2978 (−2.3830)	−.1240 (−1.7319)	.8554 (12.5529)	.903
	log D	$-.1245(10)^{1}$ (−1.0741)	.3343 (1.4860)		−.1497 (−.6753)	−.3123 (−2.4748)	.7572 (12.0124)	.833
Wholesaling	log γ	−.9544 (−2.0377)	.1499 (2.1250)		−.1226 (−2.0460)	$-.9226(10)^{-1}$ (−1.6932)	.9969 (18.7097)	.939
	log D	−.2373 (−.2780)	.1518 (1.0848)		$-.9531(10)^{-1}$ (−.6707)	$-.1583(10)^{-1}$ (−1.3432)	.8610 (14.6125)	.909

Table 21. Log Linear Regressions for Parameters of Equilibrium-Density Functions

Dependent variable		Constant term	Log population	Log SMSA median family income	Log SMSA sector employment	Log time
Population	log γ^{*}	$.9508(10)^{1}$	−.2966	$.1070(10)^{1}$		$.1483(10)^{1}$
	log D^{*}	$.8519(10)^{1}$	$.8143(10)^{-1}$	$.3018(10)^{-1}$		−.2365
Manufacturing	log γ^{*}	$-.1042(10)^{1}$	−.3554		.2904	.7706
	log D^{*}	$-.6043(10)^{1}$	.5114		.7502	−.4584
Retailing	log γ^{*}	$-.1101(10)^{1}$	.5738		−.6277	$-.1966(10)^{1}$
	log D^{*}	$-.9857(10)^{1}$	$-.1274(10)^{1}$		$-.1456(10)^{1}$	−.9660
Services	log γ^{*}	$-.1057(10)^{2}$	$.2171(10)^{1}$		$-.2046(10)^{1}$	−.8514
	log D^{*}	$-.5128(10)^{1}$	$.1377(10)^{1}$		−.6165	$-.1286(10)^{1}$
Wholesaling	log γ^{*}	$-.2998(10)^{3}$	$.4708(10)^{2}$		$-.3851(10)^{2}$	$-.2898(10)^{2}$
	log D^{*}	$-.1708(10)^{1}$	$.1092(10)^{1}$		−.6857	−.1139

As should be expected, the adjustment process is quite slow for both γ and D. In the linear equations for γ, for example, the coefficients of lagged γ average about 0.75, indicating that only about one-fourth of any deviation from equilibrium is corrected during a five-year period. And it is not surprising to learn that service employment adjusts faster than other employment categories and than population. Retailing is the next fastest category to adjust, and manufacturing and wholesaling are slowest. Population adjusts about as slowly to disequilibrium as manufacturing. The logarithmic equations show much the same ranking of sectors by speed of adjustment to disequilibrium, except that wholesaling adjusts much more slowly than any other sector. The expectation that service and retail employment might adjust most rapidly is based on the belief that less construction or movement of capital is involved in their movement than in other sectors. However, it is not clear why wholesaling should be particularly slow to adjust to disequilibrium.

If the signs of the coefficients reported in the tables are accepted, they have the striking implication that the cause of the historical flattening of population density functions has been the growth of urban population and income rather than the passage of time or whatever it stands for. The equations imply that, if population and income remained constant, urban population would become more, rather than less, concentrated. Table 19 indicates that the equilibrium value of the population γ would increase by about 0.25 per decade, or half its sample average, if population and income remained constant. Table 21 indicates that, in the logarithmic equation, the equilibrium population γ would increase by about 0.15 per decade, or 30 percent evaluated at the sample mean, if population and income remained constant. It is difficult to evaluate the finding since it is unclear what time stands for. But it does cast serious doubt on statements by Clark and others that suburbanization is inexorably related to the passage of time. An interesting conjecture is that the passage of time stands for technical progress in the construction of tall buildings, which would certainly tend to centralize urban areas.

In the employment sector equations for γ, there is a striking sign pattern among the coefficients, which is entirely consistent between the linear and logarithmic equations. The coefficient of population is negative for manufacturing and positive for all other employment sectors. The coefficients for SMSA sector employment and time are positive for manufacturing and negative for all other employment sectors. Signs of lagged dependent variables are all positive. The implication of these equations is that manufacturing employment would become less, and other employment sectors more, suburbanized through time if SMSA population and sector employment were constant. The former observation, plus the fact that the coefficient of SMSA population is negative in the manufacturing employment equation, confirms the suggestion made above that postwar flattening of manufacturing employment density functions has resulted from the growth and suburbanization of population rather than from the growth of sector employment or the passage of time. But what about the other employment sectors? The equations in tables 18 and 20 indicate that postwar flattening of employment density functions in retailing, services, and wholesaling has been caused by the growth of SMSA sector employment and the passage of time rather than by the growth of SMSA population. Why should coefficients have opposite signs in the manufacturing sector from those in the other sectors? And how does one rationalize the sign pattern in the nonmanufacturing sectors? I have no satisfactory answers to these questions. That the passage of time should result in flattening of density functions is not surprising, but it is not clear why the effect is in the opposite direction in manufacturing. That the growth of sector employment causes flattening can also be rationalized, but why should population growth have the opposite effect? The only substantial correlations among the independent variables are those between SMSA employment in the various sectors and population. These are all in excess of 0.95, and the coefficients of SMSA population and sector employment are therefore unreliable. But it is intriguing that the signs are the same in all the nonmanufacturing employment sectors and, except for that of the lagged dependent variable, exactly the opposite in the manufacturing sector.

The sign pattern among coefficients in the equations for D is much more complex. Signs of coefficients differ from one nonmanufacturing employment sector to another. More important, in some cases the sign of a particular coefficient differs as between the linear and logarithmic equations. Of course, the intuitive appeal of the model is somewhat less strong as an explanation of D than of γ. Indeed, some researchers have not even included D in their attempts to explain shifts in density functions.

APPENDIX TO CHAPTER 3

In section 1, it was indicated that Muth [26] had estimated population density function for forty-six large urbanized areas. Thirteen of Muth's cities were among the eighteen for which density functions were estimated in section 3. (The eighteen SMSAs were chosen before I had seen Muth's work.) The thirteen common estimates are presented in appendix table 3–1.

It is disappointing that only six of the estimates differ by no more than 0.10. The following facts are presumed to account for the differences.

Appendix Table 3–1. Density Gradients

City	Mills	Muth	Difference
Baltimore	0.48	0.52	−0.04
Boston	0.27	0.30	−0.03
Columbus	0.76	0.19	+0.57
Denver	0.57	0.33	+0.24
Houston	0.37	0.28	+0.09
Milwaukee	0.46	0.44	+0.02
Philadelphia	0.30	0.40	−0.10
Pittsburgh	0.27	0.09	+0.18
Rochester	0.70	0.64	+0.06
Sacramento	0.72	0.36	+0.36
San Diego	0.25	0.39	−0.14
Toledo	0.80	0.20	+0.60
Wichita	0.96	0.53	+0.43

a. The years are different. Muth's estimates are based on 1950 census data, whereas those in this study are based on estimates of the 1948 population obtained by linear interpolation between 1940 and 1950 census data. The period 1948–54 saw rapid shifts in density functions. In six of the seven SMSAs for which appendix table 3–1 estimates differ by more than 0.10, my 1954 estimates are closer to Muth's than my 1948 estimates.

b. Muth's estimates are based on samples of census tracts from the central cities, whereas mine are based on population data for the entire SMSA. Muth's data are therefore from a truncated part of the SMSA.

c. My estimation procedure, unlike Muth's, implicitly assumes that population density approaches zero asymptotically with distance from the city center. In fact, SMSAs extend a finite distance from the center of the central city, and rural population density is positive beyond that point, although it varies from the environs of one SMSA to those of another. This causes my estimates of γ to be biased upward, i.e., for my gradients to be too steep.[1] It would be possible to avoid the bias if we knew the boundaries of the urbanized portions of SMSAs, but they are known (from data on urbanized areas) only for census years since 1950. It can be seen from the final column in appendix table 3–1 that my estimates are larger than Muth's on the average.

d. Both methods involve subjective procedures in the measurement of distances and areas on maps.

1. This was pointed out to me by Richard Muth in correspondence.

4

A Survey of Some Models of
Urban Growth and Structure

During the 1960s there emerged a diffuse but substantial literature of formal models of urban development and structure. Although some good work has been done by economists, the subject is by no means economists' preserve. City planners and others have also made important contributions. But the multidisciplinary nature of the subject would make a complete and thorough survey a difficult task indeed.

A major part of the problem is to collect adequate descriptions of models. Not only is research reported in books and journals in several disciplines, but also many of the models are either inadequately reported or not reported at all in the scholarly literature. Some models have been formulated to meet the needs of public agencies in particular cities, and only a cursory description may be publicly available. And some models have been formulated on contract between public and private groups and are treated as proprietary by one or both parties to the contract. Although one cannot judge the quality of unavailable material, the sample of unpublished models I have seen reaffirms my faith in the publication process as a method of filtering out materials not worth scrutiny.

Perhaps more important, each discipline has its own terminology, interests, and preconceptions about the way the world works. Even if everyone agreed about the basic mechanisms at work, models of urban structure would be formulated differently for different purposes. For example, a model designed to portray the effects of zoning changes would differ from one designed to portray effects of changes in the urban transportation system. But there is by no means agreement concerning the basic mechanisms. City planners differ systematically from economists in the most fundamental conceptions as to the working of markets for urban land. And this difference pervades formal models, making comparison difficult.

Finally, in contrast with other specialties in economics, there have been few attempts to survey the literature on urban growth and structure.

59

The most useful surveys are by Lowry [17] and Harris [11], but both are now several years old. Many economists are unfamiliar with even the better urban models.

The purpose of this chapter is to survey a selection of urban models. The strategy has been to select a few models that are fully reported in the literature, are relatively explicit, and seem to be imaginative and relevant to the models developed in later chapters of this book. No attempt has been made at completeness, and hardly any effort has been made to obtain proprietary or other unpublished material.

1. Some General Comments

Lowry [17] has proposed a paradigm for models of urban land allocation that provides a good starting point. He assumes that an urban area is divided into a finite set of potential sites. The easiest way to imagine this being done is to suppose that public authorities lay out a lattice of streets and divide the spaces between streets into sites. Lowry supposes that each site can be occupied by only one, or no, user and that each user can occupy only one, or no, site. In fact, of course, neither assumption is literally true. Several users can occupy a given site if a tall building sits on it, and a single user may find it advantageous to occupy several contiguous sites. Each site is distinguished by its location and by other characteristics such as topography.

Lowry next supposes that there is a finite number of establishments, such as businesses and households of various types, that are potential users of the sites. From conditions for profit and utility maximization each establishment calculates the maximum rent it is willing to pay for each site. These maximum rents constitute a matrix of rent offers by each establishment for each site. Lowry assumes that the rent-offer matrix is known by site and establishment owners and that each site goes to the establishment that offers the highest rent for that site. This allocation criterion is incomplete in two respects. First, it does not indicate how ties are broken, e.g., if two establishments offer the same rent for a given site. Second, a single establishment may offer the highest rent for several or, conceivably, all sites. Then some additional allocation criteria are needed.

Much more important, Lowry's allocation rule does not follow from any assumptions explicitly in the model. Although site owners would prefer Lowry's allocation to any other, establishment owners are indifferent among all sites if they pay the rents in the rent-offer matrix. Suppose, for example, that I am an establishment owner, that my rent offers for sites one and two are 15 and 12, and that Lowry's criterion allocates my establishment to site one. Next, suppose that no other establishment can offer more than 10 for site two, and that its owner offers it to me for 11. Then I would clearly prefer site two to site one and its owner would prefer me as a tenant to other establishments. To get Lowry's result, stronger assumptions are needed.

But the most serious criticism of Lowry's paradigm is that it omits a crucial aspect of urban location. As was discussed in chapter 1, an advantage of agglomeration is that proximity facilitates exchange of goods, services, and information. Since the cost of exchange is an increasing function of distance between the parties, the rent offer of a particular establishment for a particular site depends on where other establishments are located. For example, the amount I will offer for a particular residential site depends on how far away I work. In general, the rent offer of establishment i for location j depends not only on i and j but also on the locations of some or all other establishments.

If the rent offer of establishment i for location j is assumed to depend on the locations of other establishments, Lowry's model becomes, with appropriate changes in terminology, a general description of an n-person, nonzero sum game. Establishment and site owners are players and rents are payoffs. The payoff to each player depends on his strategy and on the strategies chosen by other players.

Having stated the problem of spatial allocation in this way, it is easy to see why it is an inappropriate description of the problem. First, there is no agreement among game theorists about the fundamental characteristics of a solution to such a general game. Second, even if a solution could be characterized, the dimensions of the model in even a small city are such that the solution could not be computed and practically nothing could be said about its properties. Third, the informational requirements on the players are such that they could not compute their strategies any more than the game theorist's computer could. Fourth, realistically, the degree of simultaneity in urban location decisions is much less than is suggested by Lowry's paradigm. If one takes into account long-run allocation decisions, involving the construction, alteration, or demolition of structures, then many establishments need not consider seriously many sites, because they must pay not only the land rent being paid by the existing user but also the costs of altering or demolishing the existing structure. If one considers short-run allocation decisions in which establishments bid for the use of existing structures, simultaneity is also less than in the paradigm. An owner of an assembly line manufacturing plant need not think very seriously about the amount he would be willing to offer to rent a high floor in a modern office building.

The game theory paradigm for the urban location problem is useful as a starting point from which to classify ways in which scholars have attempted to simplify the problem in order to describe or approximate market allocation of urban land. There are two quite different ways in which model builders have attempted to simplify the problem.

The first way is by aggregation. If individual sites are aggregated into large areas, and establishments into large groups of users, the problem can become manageable. Spatial aggregation has been carried to quarter-mile-, half-mile-, or mile-square grids, to census tracts, or to the extreme of the city-suburb dichotomy. Establishments can be aggregated into more or less homogeneous groups of users such as manufacturing firms, households, and retailers.

The second procedure is to move in the opposite direction, i.e., to disaggregate sites. If we think of sites becoming smaller, then at the limit space becomes continuously variable, and the rent offer of a particular establishment or group of establishments becomes a function of continuous spatial variables. The usual procedure is then to assume or prove that rent offers follow some simple or systematic pattern. By far the most common pattern is the one in which the only relevant property of a site is its distance from the city center. In this way, it is often possible to derive very simple results about the spatial distribution of urban economic activities by making use of the calculus of maxima and minima.

The two paragraphs above are meant to indicate tendencies of model builders rather than mutually exclusive alternatives. Various combinations of the two alternatives are possible. For example, one can aggregate establishments into a small number of sectors and disaggregate sites into a spatial continuum. Likewise, a spatial pattern of rent offers could be imposed on a discrete as well as on a continuous representation of space.

An important distinction is between static and dynamic models of urban spatial allocation. As is true of nonspatial general equilibrium models, spatial models may characterize either an equilibrium configuration or the path by which the system approaches equilibrium. As is also true of nonspatial models, dynamic spatial models may be intended to portray either a literal historical sequence by which markets move toward equilibrium or a figurative process by which markets compute an equilibrium solution. Sometimes a model may be given either interpretation and it may not be clear which the author intended. But some dynamic urban models are clearly intended to portray historical processes.

Some needless controversy has arisen concerning static and dynamic spatial models. It is sometimes claimed, especially by those who are not economists, that structures are so long-lived, and movements to equilibrium therefore so slow, that static models are uninformative. But the conclusion does not follow. Generally, a well-formulated equilibrium model is a precondition for a useful dynamic model, and characteristics of equilibrium positions tell us something about the dynamic adjustment. For example, it is reasonable to argue that the gradual flattening of population and employment density functions that was studied in the previous chapter has been a response to shifting equilibrium density patterns. It is generally not possible to estimate either the deviation from equilibrium or the direction and speed of adjustment without the help of a model of the equilibrium position. The correct relationship between static and dynamic models is that both are important, and that they are complementary rather than competitive.

Models are, of course, constructed for a variety of purposes, and his purpose rightly affects the model builder's strategy. Some models are intended to be general purpose, which means that they are intended to shed light on the overall development and spatial structure of the urban area as well as to be useful for specific policy purposes. But given the limitations of data, computer memories, and human resources, general purpose models can hardly be satisfactory. Models intended to be useful for a large number of purposes usually end up being unsatisfactory for all purposes.

Models designed for limited purposes usually fall into one of three categories. But, like biological species, some urban models are hard to classify.

a. The most common kinds of models are those that provide insight into the spatial structure of urban areas. They try to show how markets allocate land to employment and housing, and how market forces affect the amounts and locations of each activity in the urban area.

b. The most difficult kind of model to formulate is one that forecasts the overall growth of urban areas. Such models pay only minimal attention to the spatial structure of the urban area.

c. A third kind of model is the public policy model. The purpose of such models is to understand the effects of public policies on urban areas. The major policy instruments sometimes considered are zoning, real estate taxation, the location of public utilities, building codes, and transportation facilities.

2. Models of Urban Growth and Structure

a. Although theoretical analysis of urban structure predates the decade of the 1960s, this survey, which will be chronological, starts with Lowdon Wingo's 1961 model [36], since it is the first of an important group of lineally related models. Wingo's model is static and space is assumed to be continuous. He focuses on the way urban transportation cost affects land rent and the residential demand for land.

Wingo assumes that the demand per household for land for residential purposes depends on the rental value of land and that the elasticity of demand is constant. He then assumes that outlay on land at any point in the urban area equals the difference between transportation cost to the city center from the edge of the urban area and that from the point in question. In other words, marginal land, at the farthest point from which people travel to the city center, has a rent of zero and land closer to the city center commands a rent equal to the saving in transportation cost. Transportation cost to the city center depends on the point from which the trip starts and on the total population of the urban area. The total amount of land available for residential use is a function of distance from the center and is exogenous at each distance. The model is completed by a relationship that equates the demand and supply of residential land in the entire urban area.

A technical issue in the analysis has to do with the correct condition for locational equilibrium. Wingo's condition equates the saving in transportation cost to outlay per household on land. As Alonso [1], writing after Wingo, has shown, the correct condition for locational equilibrium is that it not be possible to increase utility by any combination of change in location and changes in consumption of goods and services. In a model in which land (or housing services) and commuting are the only goods and in which all commuting costs are budgetary, Wingo's condition is the correct one. In a more general model in which there are other goods and services and in which some commuting costs are nonbudgetary (e.g., forgone leisure), other equations may be better approximations to the correct one. One such approximation, used in later chapters, is that a change in location should not make possible a reduction of the sum of expenditures for commuting and a given purchase of housing services.

Let $R(u)$ be rent per acre at a distance u from the city center, $f[R(u)]$ be the demand for residential land per household, and $p(u)$ be the price of transportation per commuter mile at u. Then Wingo's condition can be written

(a.1) $$f[R(u)]R(u) + \int_o^u \cdot p(u')du' = K.$$

Indeed, this is the household's budget constraint in the first of the two situations defined above. The alternative condition referred to above can be written

(a.2) $$f[R(u)]R'(u) + p(u) = 0.$$

That Wingo's condition (a.1) is different from (a.2) can be seen by differentiating (a.1) with respect to u as

(a.3) $$f'[R(u)]R(u)R'(u) + f[R(u)]R'(u) + p(u) = 0,$$

which is the same as (a.2) only if $f'[R(u)] = 0$, i.e., if housing demand is independent of price.

Wingo's assumption leads to an implausible conclusion. He assumes that the elasticity of housing demand is a constant, in which case (a.3) can be written

(a.4) $$(e + 1)f[R(u)]R'(u) + p(u) = 0,$$

where $e = f'[R(u)]R(u)/f[R(u)]$, the constant housing demand elasticity. If $e < -1$, i.e., demand is elastic, then the coefficient of the first term in (a.4) is negative. Therefore $R'(u)$ must be positive and households far from the city center consume less housing and pay a higher price for housing than households close to the city center. If $e = -1$, outlay per household on housing is independent of distance from the center and Wingo's equation cannot be satisfied unless commuting costs are zero. In fact, there is dispute as to the price elasticity of housing demand. Muth [26] estimates that it is about -1.

b. In 1963, Niedercorn [27] proposed one of the first formal dynamic models of urban growth and structure. His model is highly aggregated over space, distinguishing only between central city and suburb, but rather disaggregated among establishments, distinguishing population and seven employment sectors. The model falls naturally into two parts.

Part one consists of three equations that determine the growth of population and equilibrium and actual manufacturing employment in the urban area as a whole. The three equations are:

(b.1) $$M_e^s = \alpha_{11} P^s,$$

(b.2) $$\frac{\Delta M^s}{M^s} = \alpha_{21} \left(\frac{M_e^s - M^s}{M^s} \right) + \alpha_{22} \left(\frac{\Delta M^s}{M_{t-1}^s} \right),$$

(b.3) $$\frac{\Delta P^s}{P^s} = \alpha_{31} \left(\frac{\Delta M^s}{M^s} \right) + \alpha_{32}.$$

In this model, manufacturing employment, M, is assumed to measure basic employment, in the sense in which that term has long been used by urban specialists, and its equilibrium level, M_e^s, is assumed to be proportionate to population, P^s, as in (b.1). This superscript s means that the variable refers to the entire SMSA. The second equation says that the annual percentage change in actual manufacturing employment is a linear function of the percentage deviation of actual manufacturing employment from equilibrium and of the lagged dependent variable. The third equation says that the percentage change in population is a linear function of the percentage change in manufacturing employment.

The role of manufacturing or basic employment is unclear in this model. Niedercorn, like most writers on the subject, uses the term basic employment to refer to employment in production of goods that are exported from the urban area. In most models, the purpose of the distinction is that basic employment is exogenous in a model of a single urban area. But manufacturing employment is endogenous in Niedercorn's model, the endogenous variables in (b.1)–(b.3) being M_e^s, M^s, and P^s.

Equations (b.1)–(b.3) constitute a complex dynamic model. Niedercorn does not discuss its solution, but certain properties of the solution can be established easily. First, the model cannot possess a stationary solution in which $M^s = M_e^s = \bar{M}$ and $P^s = \bar{P}$. Substitution of these conditions into (b.1)–(b.3) yields $\alpha_{32} = 0$. Second, a similar calculation shows that no balanced growth solution, in which each variable grows at a constant geometric rate, is possible. Most important, no solution is possible in which $M_e^s = M^s$. This can be seen as follows: substituting $M_e^s = M^s$ in (b.2) implies

$$\frac{\Delta M^s}{M^s} = \alpha_{22} \left(\frac{\Delta M^s}{M^{s\,t-1}} \right),$$

which says that the growth rate of manufacturing employment goes either to zero or to infinity, depending on the value of α_{22}. But $M_e^s = M^s$ and (b.1) imply that the growth rates of population and manufacturing employment are equal. Then, (b.3) implies

$$\frac{\Delta M^s}{M^s} = \frac{\alpha_{32}}{1 - \alpha_{31}},$$

which says that the growth rate of manufacturing employment must be a constant and is inconsistent with the equation above. The implication is that manufacturing employment cannot start in equilibrium, be in equilibrium, or approach equilibrium as long as the model holds. It is unclear what role the notion of equilibrium employment plays in the model.

Part two consists of equations that determine central city and suburban population, manufacturing employment, and demand-oriented employment.

Central city manufacturing employment and population are determined by the following two equations:[1]

(b.4) $\Delta M^c = \alpha_{41} \left(\dfrac{V}{L} \right) \left(\dfrac{M^c}{M^s} \right) \Delta M_g^s + \alpha_{42} \left(\dfrac{M^c}{M^s} \right) \Delta M_d^s + \alpha_{43}.$

(b.5) $\Delta P^c = \alpha_{51} \left(\dfrac{V}{L} \right) \left(\dfrac{P^c}{P^s} \right) \Delta P^s + \alpha_{52} \left(\dfrac{P^c}{L} \right) P^c + \alpha_{53}.$

Here the superscript c stands for the central city and V and L are vacant

---

1. Terms that account for population annexation by the central city have been omitted in the presentation here.

and total land in the central city. ΔM_g^s and ΔM_d^s are defined as follows:

$$\Delta M_g^s = \begin{cases} \Delta M^s & \text{if } \Delta M^s > 0 \\ 0 & \text{if } \Delta M^s \leq 0 \end{cases} \qquad \Delta M_d^s = \begin{cases} \Delta M^s & \text{if } \Delta M^s < 0 \\ 0 & \text{if } \Delta M^s \geq 0 \end{cases}$$

The idea here is that, when SMSA manufacturing employment is growing, growth of central city manufacturing employment is inhibited if vacant land is scarce, whereas if SMSA manufacturing employment is shrinking, central city shrinkage is not inhibited by the availability of vacant land. Equations (b.4) and (b.5) assert that changes in manufacturing employment and population will be allocated between central city and suburbs in proportion to existing manufacturing employment and population, except insofar as scarcity of vacant land prevents it.

The location of each of six categories of demand-oriented employment, E, is determined by equations of the following form:

(b.6) $\qquad \Delta E^c = \alpha_{61} \Delta P^c + \alpha_{62} \Delta P^r + \alpha_{64}.$

(b.7) $\qquad \Delta E^r = \alpha_{71} \Delta P^r + \alpha_{73}.$

The superscript r refers to location in the suburban ring around the central city.

Equations (b.4)–(b.7) are all subject to the criticism that the model contains no mechanism to ensure consistency between its two geographical parts and the urban area as a whole. In (b.4) and (b.5) there is nothing that ensures that central city manufacturing employment and population will stay between zero and the totals for the SMSA. Equation (b.6) asserts that annual changes in demand-oriented central city employment will continue indefinitely at α_{64} even if central city and suburban-ring populations are constant; (b.7) has the same implication for suburban employment. In other words, these employment categories might eventually become either extremely large or extremely small in relationship to the population they serve.

c. In 1964, Alonso [1] provided the most complete and general model of urban location theory. The model is static and, in its most general form, assumes an arbitrarily large number of different kinds of firms and households. Urban space is taken to be continuous and one-dimensional in that the only relevant dimension is distance from the center. Alonso does not say why distance from the center is important, but the presumption is that jobs and sales are located there.

The first part of Alonso's book develops the theory of the consumer and the firm in a spatial context. Households maximize utility, which depends on three variables: goods (which can be interpreted as a vector);

housing; and distance from the city center. Distance can represent the utility of living in a low-density neighborhood or nonmonetary costs of commuting. Prices of goods and housing are independent of amounts bought. The price of goods is also independent of location, but the price of housing and commuting costs depend on distance. The budget constraint equates the sum of expenditures on goods, housing, and commuting to the exogenous income of the household. The household maximizes utility with respect to goods, housing, and distance, subject to the budget constraint. The maximization conditions yield a function, called the bid price, showing the land rent the household could pay at each distance in order to achieve a predetermined utility level. At each point on the bid-price curve, goods and housing are, of course, adjusted to maximize utility. There is a bid-price curve for each utility level. Alonso uses the term "price structure" to designate the functions showing the market price of land at each distance from the city center. Under certain restrictions on the shapes of the bid-price and price-structure curves, the household's equilibrium location is determined by tangency between the two. Interpretation is analogous to that of tangency between a budget line and indifference curve in the nonspatial theory of consumer behavior.

The theory of the firm starts by defining profit as total revenue minus the sum of land and nonland production costs. Revenue and nonland costs depend on quantity sold and on location. Land rent is exogenous to the firm but depends on distance from the center. Land cost equals land rent multiplied by the quantity of land demanded. Having started the theory of consumer behavior with the utility function, Alonso might have started the theory of the firm with the production function, but the model could easily be reformulated for that purpose. The firm maximizes profits with respect to quantity produced and location. Analogously with the household's bid price, the firm's bid price is the function showing land rent at each distance that will yield a given total profit, given that the profit-maximizing output is produced at each location. Again, locational equilibrium is determined at the point of tangency between the price structure and the firm's bid price.

In the second part of the book, Alonso develops the theory of market equilibrium for the urban land market. The conditions for market equilibrium are that each land user's bid price be tangent to the price structure, where the price structure is the envelope of bid prices, and that supply and demand for land be equal. Most attention is devoted to the case in which each establishment's (i.e., firm's or household's) bid prices constitute a family of parallel straight lines. Slopes may differ from establishment to establishment. In this situation, Alonso concludes that establishments will be ranked by distance from the city center according to the rank by steepness of their bid prices, the establishments with steeper bid prices being closer to the center.

It is easy to show that Alonso's assumptions are not strong enough to establish the conclusion. Consider the simplest case, emphasized by Alonso, in which there are two establishments and two locations. No more than one establishment can be at one location. Alonso's argument can be shown with the aid of figure 1 (adapted from [1], p. 78). $R_A(u)$ and $R_B(u)$ are bid prices of establishments A and B, and 1 and 2 are the locations. Assume that $R_B(u)$ is flatter than $R_A(u)$ and consider the member of each family, intersecting above 2, shown in the figure. Alonso claims that A will locate at 1 and B at 2, because, $R_A(u)$ being steeper than $R_B(u)$, $R_A(1) > R_B(1)$, and A can therefore outbid B for 1. Alonso also claims that the price structure for the two sites will be $R_A(1)$ and $R_B(2) = R_A(2)$, because landlords can charge land rents as high as these without fear of losing customers.

The analysis breaks down because these bid prices are members of their families, chosen arbitrarily except for the restriction that they intersect above 2. But an infinity of pairs of bid prices satisfies this restriction. Until we know something about the utility and profit levels they represent, we can say nothing about who will locate where. To clarify the situation, consider the highest bid prices of the two establishments at which they will locate in the urban areas at all. At land rents above these levels they would

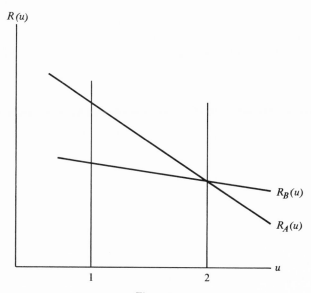

Figure 1.

prefer to locate elsewhere or not at all. Call these bid prices $R_A^o(u)$ and
$R_B^o(u)$ and consider those shown in figure 2. In the case shown, B can outbid A for either site and nothing in the analysis tells us which he will
choose. Which location B prefers depends on how far land rents are below
$R_B^o(1)$ and $R_B^o(2)$. Which location A prefers depends on how far they are
below $R_A^o(1)$ and $R_A^o(2)$. Alonso's contention to the contrary notwithstand-
ing, the establishments have strong incentives to offer rents below their bid
prices. Landlords have no uses for the sites other than renting them to the
two establishments and would therefore prefer renting to not renting at
any positive rent. Nothing follows from the analysis other than that land
rents will be between zero and the larger of R_A^o and R_B^o. Literature on game
theory and oligopoly suggests several sets of assumptions that could be
made about information available to the establishments and about the
strategies they choose. Each set of assumptions would lead to a specific land
allocation. But they are not made by Alonso.

The fact is that Alonso has defined a rather general game, not sig-
nificantly more specialized than the Lowry paradigm discussed in the
previous section. If one permits coalitions, one gets one class of solutions.
If one permits randomized strategies but not coalitions, one gets another
class of strategies. If one permits neither, then nothing ensures or even
suggests that a saddle point exists for minmax strategies. Finally, nothing
in the above analysis depends on there being only two establishments and
two sites. The criticisms therefore apply to the general case analyzed by
Alonso starting on page 82 of his book.

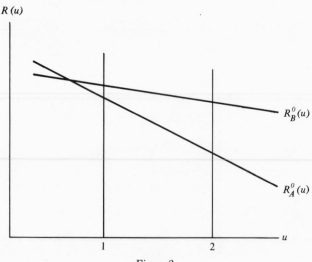

Figure 2.

It seems clear that Alonso has taken over the conclusions, but not the assumptions, from the analysis that he and others have undertaken concerning agricultural location. In that application, bid prices are derived from maximizing behavior in a way similar to that described above, and it is assumed that there is a finite number of different kinds of establishments (e.g., growers of different kinds of crops). But it is assumed that there is an indefinitely large supply of establishments of each kind, each among a kind having the same family of bid price functions. Then each site would be rented to the kind of establishment whose $R^o(u)$ was greatest at that u. And no landlord would rent a site for less than the largest $R^o(u)$, since, if he did, another establishment of the same kind would be willing to pay a higher rent. With these assumptions, all of Alonso's results follow.

The additional assumptions needed to get Alonso's results are of course those that ensure perfect competition. They are reasonable assumptions in many urban models, and they are used in the models in subsequent chapters. Furthermore, within their confines, Alonso's is the most comprehensive analysis available in the literature. But I believe Alonso was wrong to conclude he could derive the results from his much less stringent assumptions.

A second criticism is that Alonso's bid prices are derived on the implicit assumption that employment is in the city center. At least there is no formal analysis of the case in which one sector's bid prices depend on the locations of other sectors. Yet among the sectors whose locations are to be determined by the model are employment sectors. Then it cannot be assumed that all employment is in the city center and locations of housing and employment must be determined simultaneously.

d. In 1964, Lowry [16] published one of the first large discrete models of spatial relationships in a metropolitan area. It is still the best available model of its type. The model is static, but the iterative solution procedure might be given a dynamic interpretation.

Lowry estimated and solved the model for the Pittsburgh metropolitan area. He divided the metropolitan area into 456 tracts, each with about one square mile of land area. There are three sectors in the model: the basic, or export, sector; the retail, or locally oriented, sector; and housing. The variables in the model are housing, sectoral employment, and land use in each tract. In each tract the amounts of land and employment in the basic sector are exogenous.

Retail employment[2] in each tract is determined by total employment

2. Lowry's model contains several retail sectors. For simplicity of exposition, it is assumed here that there is only one.

in that tract and by population resident in that and other tracts:

(d.1) $$E_j^R = b^R\left[C^R\sum_i \frac{N_i}{T_{ij}} + d^R E_j \right].$$

Here, E_j^R is retail employment in tract j, E_j is total employment in tract j, and N_i is population in tract i. T_{ij} is a measure of transportation cost between tracts i and j. The constants b^R, C^R, and d^R are to be determined by the data. The idea behind (d.1) is that employees in tract j make shopping trips in tract j but not to other tracts, whereas residents in tract i make shopping trips to all tracts, but with frequency that is inversely proportional to T_{ij}. Equation (d.1) is related to so-called "gravity models," in which it is assumed that interactions (in this case shopping) are proportional to mass (in this case population) and inversely proportional to distance (in this case T_{ij}) or, more commonly, its square.

Population in each tract is determined in a manner analogous to (d.1), i.e., it depends on access to employment:

(d.2) $$N_j = g\sum_i \frac{E_i}{T_{ij}}.$$

Population and employment are thus simultaneously determined.

Additional equations state that land used for retailing is proportional to retail employment in each tract, that total retail employment is a fixed proportion of total population and that total employment is a fixed proportion of total population. Total employment is employment summed over sectors and tracts, and total population is population summed over tracts. An inequality ensures that retailing not take place on a very small scale in any tract, i.e., it ensures that retail employment either be zero or exceed a minimum level. Another inequality ensures that population density on land devoted to housing not exceed a predetermined level. Finally, total usable land in each tract must be at least as great as that used for basic and retail employment and housing.

Economically, Lowry's model is very simple. Basic employment in each tract is exogenous. Retail employment and population in each tract are determined simultaneously by (d.1) and (d.2). The rest of the model consists of identities, inequality constraints, and equilibrium conditions for the metropolitan area as a whole. However, the data and data processing demands of the system are enormous.

The asymmetry between the assumptions about land use for employment and population is worth noting. Land use per employee is a constant, whereas population density is restricted only by an inequality. The model assumes that, up to the stipulated maximum, people are indifferent to density regardless of income. There is considerable evidence to the contrary, but alternatives would probably be difficult to build into the model.

To make sense, the two gravity equations (d.1) and (d.2) must be interpreted as demand equations. Economists are inclined to say that gravity models are implausible demand equations. Certainly they are different from the equations that determine locational equilibrium in the work of Wingo and Alonso. But in those models, location is specified by one variable, distance from the center. In Lowry's model, location depends on both distance and direction. It is thus a much more complex model, and economists have not yet worked out locational conditions for such a model. There is no reason to think they would resemble the gravity model, but until we have more complete theoretical analysis, the issue is mainly one of descriptive accuracy. Presumably, the appropriate theoretical analysis would represent trade-offs between housing costs and transportation costs to places of work and shopping centers.

The basic or export sector always causes problems in urban models. It is reasonable to assume that employment in production of export goods is exogenous. But of course, as in international trade, some of the same goods may be consumed locally. It is therefore a much stronger assumption that total employment in the industries producing export goods is exogenous. And it is a stronger assumption yet that the location of export goods production is exogenous within the urban area. Presumably, export goods producers are affected by the set of trade-offs between central city and suburban locations that affect other employers. Intra-urban area location of manufacturing employment is among the most important issues regarding suburbanization, and it would be interesting to try to gain insight into the process using a model like Lowry's.

To conclude this subsection, reference should be made to a direct descendent of Lowry's model, published by Crecine [6] in 1968. Crecine's model is considerably more disaggregated and computationally complex than Lowry's, but it makes use of very similar economic notions.

e. Chapin and his coworkers at the University of North Carolina have developed a series of urban models. References to earlier reports are in a 1968 summary article by Chapin and Weiss [4], on which this review is mainly based. The model described here was estimated and tested with data for Greensboro, North Carolina. The focus of the model is the effects of public policies on residential development. The model is discrete and dynamic. Iterations are intended to represent historical development of the urban area.

Chapin and Weiss divide the urban area into a grid, each of whose cells contains about twenty-three acres of land. These cells are much smaller than Lowry's, presumably because Chapin and Weiss's urban area is much smaller than Lowry's and therefore smaller cells can be used without the computer capacity's being exceeded because of the number of cells.

Chapin and Weiss use multiple regression analysis to estimate the effect of predetermined variables on residential development in the cells. In the final regression, historical development in each cell is regressed on seven variables: land not in urban use, accessibility to work areas, assessed value of land, travel distance to nearest major street, distance to nearest elementary school, residential amenity, and availability of sewerage. The authors estimate time lags by choosing those with the greatest explanatory value.

The model is applied to a historical period as follows: At any time, say 1948, the numbers and locations of population and employment are ascertained. On the basis of these data and of values of the exogenous variables, the attractiveness of each cell for further development is computed. Then the growth of population in the urban area and the growth and location of employment in each cell during the next three years are treated as exogenous. The exogenous population growth is allocated to cells according to the attractiveness computed with the regression equation. For the next three-year period, exogenous and predetermined variables are recomputed, and further population growth is allocated among cells in the same way. If the model were to be used to forecast future growth, forecasts of urban area population growth and of each cell's employment growth would have to be made. A forecast could then be made conditional on each set of values of public policy variables.

The Chapin-Weiss model contains much less simultaneity than the Lowry model discussed in subsection d. Lowry's model located population and retail employment simultaneously, whereas Chapin and Weiss treat all employment as predetermined. They do not therefore require an iterative computation of endogenous variables for a particular point in time.

The salient characteristic of the Chapin-Weiss model is the attempt to understand the effect of public policy variables on residential location. Unfortunately, it is unlikely that the variables they have chosen can be regarded as exogenous during the period in which they estimated their regression equations. Take distance to the nearest elementary school as an example. An extreme hypothesis is that public authorities locate elementary schools wherever residential development is occurring or is forecast to occur. Although the extreme hypothesis may not be the whole story, one would certainly hope that, whatever decision rule public authorities use to locate elementary schools, population growth in the area is included among its independent variables. And it is somewhat hard to imagine what other variables should be important. But this means that the correlation Chapin and Weiss observe between population growth and distance to an elementary school consists partly of the effect of proximity to elementary school on population growth and partly of the effect of population growth on the location of elementary schools. In other words, there are simultaneous relationships between the two variables. The result is that their regression overstates the effect of elementary school construction on population growth.

The criticism also applies to Chapin and Weiss's other public policy variables, such as distance to a main street, availability of sewerage, and assessed value of land. If assessed value is assumed to be related to market value, it must be entirely effect rather than cause of residential development. If it were a cause, e.g., because the land was valued for commercial purposes, its coefficient would be negative. Other things being equal, residential development will be less the higher the value of the land for other purposes. The fact that their estimated coefficient is positive indicates that assessed value is effect rather than cause. One hopes the city fathers are not led to believe that they can promote residential development by raising land assessments!

It is, of course, difficult to know whether one can treat public policy decisions as exogenous in models of urban development. If not, it is necessary to estimate simultaneously the supply equations of public services and the demand equations for land uses that depend, among other things, on the availability of public services. But in the absence of simultaneous equation studies that show the contrary, the presumption must be that at least the location of public services depends partly on residential and other kinds of development.

f. Muth's 1969 volume [26] must be regarded as a landmark in urban economics. It is less ambitious than other research surveyed in this chapter in that it is almost entirely concerned with housing markets and says almost nothing about location of nonhousing activities in urban areas. Much of the book is concerned with elaboration, estimation, and testing of the basic model, but this survey will be restricted to the basic model. As does Alonso, Muth has separate chapters on the equilibrium of households, suppliers of housing services, and the housing market as a whole.

Muth's theory of demand is similar to Alonso's. Household utility depends on the consumption of housing services and other commodities (which can be interpreted as a vector). Unlike Alonso, Muth does not include commuting distance in the utility function. Instead, he interprets other commodities to include leisure and his budget constraint equates "income" to expenditure on housing, transportation, and other commodities. "Income" must therefore include not only money income but also money income forgone in order to consume leisure. In this model it is a strong assumption that the price of leisure does not depend on income. Muth's procedure is motivated by the fact that the time cost of commuting is paid in part by forgone leisure and in part by forgone money income. Thus, he assumes that transportation costs depend on distance and "income." Household equilibrium conditions are obtained by maximizing utility, constrained by the budget equation, with respect to housing services, other commodities, and distance. Households behave competitively in that they assume their purchases will not affect the prices of housing services and other commodities, but the price of housing services does depend on distance.

Muth assumes that all employment is in the central business district (CBD) and distance is therefore measured from the city center. After some discussion (p. 38), he concludes that noncommuting trips to the CBD are few and mostly for luxury goods and services. The implication is that most purchases are made in residential areas, and it is therefore incongruous to assume that all employment is in the CBD. Most urban model builders, however, do not even mention noncommuting trips to the CBD.

Muth's theory of the supply of housing services starts with the assumption that all housing services are produced with the same production function, using land and nonland as inputs. Producers are competitive and assume input and output prices to be independent of amounts purchased and sold, but to depend on distance. Producers employ amounts of land and nonland inputs that maximize profits at each distance. Muth also assumes that land rents and prices of housing services are set by the markets so that profits of housing service producers are exactly zero wherever housing services are produced.

The model is completed by the assumption that the urban area extends as far as is necessary to equate demand and supply of housing services. Muth assumes that land available for housing at a distance u from the center is proportionate to u and that the factor of proportionality is exogenous. Land not used for housing is used for transportation and other purposes. Thus, land used for transportation is exogenous to the model, and transportation does not compete for land with housing and other uses. The total number of CBD workers is also exogenous.

Muth was the first writer to show the conditions under which population density will be a negative exponential function of distance from the center, as assumed by Clark and others. Muth's condition for household locational equilibrium is similar to (a.2) above:

(f.1) $$q(u)p'(u) + T_u = 0,$$

where $q(u)$ is the demand for housing services per household, $p'(u)$ is the derivative of the price of housing services with respect to distance, and T_u is commuting cost per mile at u. If all households have the same tastes and income, then (f.1) holds for each household and at each u. Muth assumes, on the basis of earlier research, that the price elasticity of demand for housing is minus one, and that commuting cost per mile is constant. Then (f.1) can be written

$$Bp(u)^{-1}p'(u) + T_u = 0,$$

where B is a multiplicative constant in the housing demand equation and T_u is a constant, and on integrating

$$p(u) = p_o e^{-ru},$$

where $r = T_u/B$. It is remarkable that this result holds regardless of supply conditions in the housing market. Muth then proceeds to show that, if the housing services production function is Cobb-Douglas with constant returns to scale, then the value of housing services per square mile of land devoted to housing declines exponentially with respect to distance. But with a unit price elasticity of demand for housing services, expenditure on housing services is proportionate to the number of households, and therefore population or household density also declines exponentially.

g. Jay Forrester's recent book [9] is not only the last but by far the most ambitious model to be surveyed in this chapter. Forrester's goal is a complete analysis of the life cycle of a city—growth, maturity, and stagnation—and a complete evaluation of the spectrum of policies intended to revive the stagnant city. To achieve his goal, Forrester employs a complex model consisting of about 150 equations, and the bulk of the book consists of presentation and analysis of computer print-outs representing numerical solutions of the model. Forrester's model bears little resemblance to earlier urban models, and there is no evidence that he was influenced by them. His model does, however, bear strong resemblance to his earlier work on industrial dynamics, and readers of his earlier book [8] will find much in the current volume that is familiar. Indeed, of the six references in the volume, five are to Forrester's earlier work.

The model is divided into twelve sectors. The first three sectors characterize labor markets for each of the three classes of employees in the model: underemployed, laborers, and managers. The next three sectors characterize housing markets for each of the three classes: under-employed housing, worker housing, and premium housing. Then there are three sectors that describe the three kinds of businesses in the model: new enterprises, mature businesses, and declining industry. The tenth sector describes the finance of public services and redistributional programs. The eleventh sector presents input-output relationships, identities, and equilibrium conditions in the labor markets. Finally, sector twelve characterizes a variety of urban development programs. The best place for the technical reader to start in this book is appendix A, where all the equations are presented and described carefully and systematically.

It is obviously not feasible to describe Forrester's model in detail. But much of the model consists of a few basic ideas applied to several sectors with relatively minor variations.

Most of the sixty-two equations that describe the three labor markets are concerned with in-migration to and out-migration from the city of the three classes of employees. Migration depends on the perceived attractive-ness of the city, which in turn depends, with a lag, on the actual attractive-ness of the city. Attractiveness depends multiplicatively on a series of multipliers representing upward mobility (movement to a higher labor force group) and the availability of housing, public services, and employ-ment to the class of employees.

The three housing markets are described in thirty-seven equations. Premium (managerial) and worker housing are constructed by the private sector. Worker housing also becomes available by filtering down from premium housing. Underemployed housing becomes available by filtering down, but it is not constructed by the private sector. All three housing types can be constructed by public renewal programs. Construction by the private sector depends on lagged desired construction, which in turn depends multiplicatively on a series of multipliers representing the ade-quacy of existing housing, land availability, housing taxes, and the growth of employment of the class in question.

The growth and decline of the three business sectors are described in twenty-one equations. New enterprises are constructed from scratch. They filter into mature businesses, and mature businesses into declining busi-nesses, at rates that depend on the functioning of the system. Declining industry is demolished at a rate that also depends on the behavior of the system. New enterprise construction is the key to the performance of the three business sectors. New enterprise construction depends on desired new enterprise construction, which in turn depends on a weighted sum of the stocks of new enterprises, mature businesses, and declining busi-nesses, the sum being multiplied by an enterprise multiplier. The enter-prise multiplier depends on the availability of managers, workers, and land as well as on business taxes and an enterprise growth multiplier. The enterprise growth multiplier is an accelerator-like term representing the effect of the new enterprise growth rate on new enterprise construction. There is also a public new enterprise construction program.

Total land in the city is fixed, and input-output coefficients determine land used per unit of the three kinds of housing and the three kinds of businesses. But locational relationships among the housing and business sectors play no role in the model. There is no mention of commuting or other urban transportation. Input-output coefficients also relate employment of the three labor force groups to production of the various kinds of business enterprises.

Starting with initial conditions thought to be appropriate for a small urban area, the computer solves the model for a 250-year life cycle of the city. The characteristic pattern is an initial period of gradually accelerating growth, followed by deceleration, and then stagnation after 200 years or so. Despite the complexity of the model, it is not very difficult to see why it produces the numerical results Forrester presents. Acceleration comes about because of the simple feedbacks in the system. For example, new enterprise construction is an increasing function of the rate of growth of new enterprises. Deceleration occurs because the total land available to the city is fixed (Forrester's city is apparently a legal city whose boundaries cannot be moved), and land scarcity eventually causes stagnation.

Forrester then computes the effects of four kinds of rather conventional programs to alleviate distress in the city: job creation in the public sector for the underemployed; a training program for the underemployed; a program of outside (presumably federal) aid to the public sector; and a low-cost housing program. Without exception the results of these programs are to leave unchanged or to worsen indexes of distress such as unemployment rates and housing shortage for the underemployed. He then computes the effects of programs to encourage industry such as public new-enterprise construction and the demolition of slums and declining businesses. These policies have almost uniformly favorable results.

It is also easy to understand why Forrester's model yields the policy evaluations he reports. They result from two basic characteristics of the model. First, there is an indefinitely large reserve army of underemployed who will migrate to the city if housing and other conditions are favorable. Therefore, attempts to improve the lot of the underemployed mainly attract more underemployed to the city until conditions are no better than before. But increased numbers of underemployed leave less room in the city for industry and therefore worsen the employment situation. Second, there is no limit on the demand side to the growth of industry in the city. Therefore, programs designed to aid industry inevitably work and alleviate unemployment and other distress signals. It is extremely doubtful whether these are appropriate assumptions on which to base the analysis of renewal policies. Certainly, they should not be used without extensive theoretical and empirical justification, not provided by Forrester.

It is hard to take Forrester's model seriously as a description of the urban economy. It contains no production functions except input-output coefficients for land and labor. It contains no factor prices and no factor markets that are recognizable to economists. It contains no output prices and no output markets. There are many ad hoc assumptions about lags, functional forms, and coefficient values. All are introduced without reference to economic theory or empirical studies. Although the model makes strong and implausible assumptions about migration, public finance, and urban labor markets, there is no indication that it has been influenced by previous work in any of these areas. Economists have not, of course, said the last word on any of these subjects, and there is no reason for Forrester to accept any specific results. But Forrester simply ignores everything economists have said about production, markets and public finance. He puts forward his own hypotheses without justification, as though their statement makes them self-evident, whereas the opposite is true.

It is tempting to say that Forrester's model is more sociological than economic, but it is equally free of reference to previous work in urban sociology and demography. The problem is certainly not that too few relationships are included. Rather, the opposite. The model is needlessly complex for Forrester's purpose. The problem is that the relationships in the model are not at all persuasive.

5

A Simple Model with Fixed
Production Coefficients

The most prominent and pervasive characteristic of urban economies in the United States is that residences are more suburbanized than production. It is clear from the most casual observation of the directions of morning and afternoon commuting traffic. In addition, the data in chapter 2 showed that, in the early 1960s, 40 percent of the residents of ninety large SMSAs lived in central cities, whereas 50 percent worked there. Further evidence is provided by the density functions in chapter 3, which show that the density of the various categories of employment fell faster with distance from the city center than did population density.

The relationship between the locations of residences and employment is a central concern of the models analyzed in subsequent chapters. In this chapter, the subject is introduced in the simplest model in which the issue can be posed.[1] The advantages of the simple model are that the most fundamental relationships are transparent and that both market and efficient resource allocations can be analyzed exhaustively. But the simple model lacks the richness and realism of more complex models.

There seem to be two significant mechanisms that account for the greater suburbanization of residences than of employment. One works through the output side and the other through the input side.

First, consider a city that exists because it is uneconomic to produce a certain commodity on a small scale. The size of the city is partly determined by the population necessary to generate enough demand to enable production to take place on an economically large scale. The city may or may not trade with the outside world. Then, wherever production is

---

1. The model in this chapter is formally similar to that analyzed in [21]. The interpretation, however, is somewhat different. More important, the results obtained in the earlier paper by control theory are derived here with nothing more than simple algebra. I am indebted to Trent Bertrand and David Bradford for persuading me that the simpler techniques would do.

located, the most economical way to distribute the output is for the customers to locate in the area surrounding the production facility. On some
assumptions about transportation, the cost of distributing the output to
customers will be minimized if residences locate in a ring like a doughnut
around the production site. In this city the location of the production
facility becomes the city center and the surrounding locations of customers
become the suburbs. The city center contains only production and the
suburbs contain only residences, so there is complete segregation of employment from residences. The model is not basically more complicated
if it is assumed that there are several goods produced with scale economies
and that they find it advantageous to locate adjacent to each other.
Segregation of employment from residence becomes partial rather than
complete if it is assumed that there are additional goods whose scale
economies are such that less than the entire population of the urban area
is required to generate sufficient demand for them to operate on an
economically large scale. Each such activity could be located in each of
several suburban subcenters. The number and locations of such subcenters
would depend on the details of assumptions concerning transportation
and scale economies. If subcenters are introduced, there will be some
completely segregated central city employment and some employment
partly integrated with residential activity. Although it is easy to lay out
the general outlines of such a model, it seems to be difficult to formulate
and solve one explicitly. As an example of the usefulness of such a model,
it is hard to imagine an adequate evaluation of zoning and other land use
controls without such a framework of analysis.

Second, consider an urban area that produces a commodity for export
to the outside world and suppose that the commodity must be sent for
export to a railroad, harbor, crossroad, or airport. In this model the
terminal or interchange constitutes the city center, and production and
residences will locate in the surrounding area. But how much more
suburbanized residences will be than production depends on additional
assumptions concerning production and transportation.

The model analyzed in this chapter contains some very simple
assumptions about production and transportation with which the second
mechanism can be analyzed. The main reason for concentrating on the
second mechanism is that it leads naturally to the more complex models
analyzed in subsequent chapters. But it is worth mentioning that the
presence of scale economies makes models of the first mechanism fundamentally more complex than those of the second mechanism. Economists
have few ideas as to the way scale economies are affected by proximity or
distance. More important, the spatial aspects of competition are subtle
and complex in models with scale economies.

The model is presented in detail in the next section. In section 2, the Pareto optimum spatial allocation is derived. In section 3, it is shown that competitive markets will reproduce the optimum allocation. In section 4, rough orders of magnitude are established for the parameters of the model. Some concluding remarks are presented in section 5.

1. THE MODEL

Two commodities are produced in the urban area under consideration. Commodity one is the export good. The number of units to be exported, X, is exogenous, and all the units must be shipped to a predetermined delivery point for export. Commodity two is housing services for workers and their families.

The geography of the urban area is such that all the land surrounding the delivery point is available for production of the two commodities, except for a pie slice of $(2\pi - \phi)$ radians, where $0 \leq \phi \leq 2\pi$.

The technology is of the simplest input-output kind. Each unit of output of commodity one requires a fixed input of land and labor. Each worker requires one unit of housing services, which is produced with a fixed input of land. Without loss of generality, we can choose units of commodity one so that one worker produces one unit of commodity one. Thus, the labor force and the production of commodities one and two are all equal to each other for the urban area as a whole.

These assumptions can be expressed as follows:

(1) $$X_1(u) = a_1 L_1(u),$$

(2) $$X_2(u) = a_2 L_2(u),$$

(3) $$L_1(u) + L_2(u) = \phi u,$$

(4) $$\int_0^{\bar{u}} X_1(u)du = \int_0^{\bar{u}} X_2(u)du = X.$$

Equations (1)–(3) hold for all u where $0 \leq u \leq \bar{u}$.

In these equations, u is the distance in miles from the delivery point for commodity one, which is the city center. $X_1(u)$ and $X_2(u)$ are the outputs of commodities one and two u miles from the delivery point. $L_1(u)$ and $L_2(u)$ are land used to produce commodities one and two u miles from the delivery point. Equations (1) and (2) express the input-output production relations between the outputs of commodities one and two and land devoted to their production. Output per acre of commodities one and two are a_1 and a_2. Equation (3) ensures that the land devoted to production equals the amount available at each u. Equation (4) states that land will be used as far away from the delivery point as is necessary to produce the required amounts of the two commodities. The greatest distance at which production will take place is $\bar{u}$; however, it is important to note that $\bar{u}$ depends only on the production coefficients, ϕ and X—it does not depend on the way land is allocated to production of the two commodities. In fact, if equations (1) and (2) are solved for $L_1(u)$ and $L_2(u)$; the results substituted into (3); and (3) is integrated using (4), it follows easily that

$$(5) \qquad \qquad \bar{u} = \left[\frac{2(a_1 + a_2)X}{a_1 a_2 \phi} \right]^{\frac{1}{2}} .$$

It is clear that the model would be basically unchanged if labor were required to produce housing services as well as the export good, and if capital were required to produce both goods, provided the input-output ratios were constants. The total outputs of the two commodities are predetermined, and therefore the total capital and labor inputs required do not depend on the way space is allocated. The additional input requirements would affect neither the market nor the efficient allocation of space.

The model is completed by introducing costs of transporting commodity one and of commuting. Let t_1 be the cost per mile of transporting a unit of commodity one, and t_2 be the cost per one mile round trip of commuting. It is assumed that transportation cost depends only on airline distance to the delivery point. Then the freight cost of a unit of commodity one is t_1 times the distance the unit is shipped, and the commuting cost for a worker is t_2 times the distance between his place of work and place of residence. If a certain fraction of the land at each u is set aside for transportation, it can be included in the $2\pi - \phi$ radians of land unavailable for production. But in this model it is assumed that the land needed for transportation of freight and commuters does not depend on the pattern of land allocation to production of exports and housing services. In subsequent chapters, this restrictive assumption is dropped, at the cost of greatly complicating the model.

In this model, only transportation costs vary with the way land is allocated. Total land and labor inputs are entirely specified by the exogenously determined output of commodity one.

2. SOLUTION OF THE PLANNING PROBLEM

In this section the Pareto optimum allocation of land is derived for the input-output model presented in the previous section. Thus, the point of view is that of the central planner who attempts to allocate land in the urban area so as to minimize the real resources absorbed in delivering X units of commodity one to the delivery point. It was shown in the previous section that only transportation costs, and not labor costs, vary with the allocation of land. Therefore, the central planner's problem is to minimize transportation costs with respect to land allocation and subject to certain constraints.

A trivial property of an efficient allocation of land is that workers should not commute away from the city center on the way to work. The reason is that outward commuting involves cross-hauling, i.e., hauling the commuter outward from the city center and then hauling back toward the center the product in which his services are embodied. If any worker's place of residence is closer to the city center than his place of work, total transportation costs can be reduced by a trade in which the outward commuter's residence is moved to his place of work and his place of work is moved to his residence. After the trade, the worker's total travel is unchanged, but he is commuting in the opposite direction, whereas the total transportation of the export good has been unambiguously reduced. If outward commuting is to be avoided the cumulative production of commodity one between the city center and any u must be at least as great as the cumulative production of commodity two in the same area. Otherwise, at least some workers would have to commute outward. The condition can be expressed mathematically as

$$(6) \qquad \int_o^u [X_1(u') - X_2(u')]du' \geq 0. \qquad\qquad 0 \leq u \leq \bar{u}$$

Equation (6) ensures that, between zero and u, there are at least as many jobs as workers' residences. There is thus no need for any worker living between zero and u to work beyond u.

If (6) holds, the total cost of transporting commodities and workers can be expressed as

$$(7) \qquad C = t_1 \int_o^{\bar{u}} u X_1(u)du + t_2 \int_o^{\bar{u}} \int_o^u [X_1(u') - X_2(u')]du'du.$$

The first term in (7) is straightforward. It says that, if $X_1(u)$ units of commodity one are produced u miles from the delivery point, they must be shipped u miles at a cost of t_1 per unit mile. The second term is somewhat more complicated. Suppose that the cumulative production of commodities one and two, as functions of u, is as shown in figure 3. The vertical distance between the two functions is the left-hand side of (6). By (6), it is positive and it shows that the number of workers that must be transported through u toward the city center is the cumulative excess of production of commodity one over production of commodity two between the city center and u. If the number of workers transported through u is multiplied by

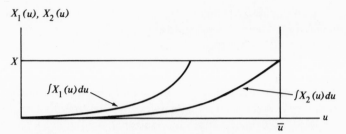

Figure 3. Cumulative Production of Commodities One and Two.

t_2du, the result is the cost of transporting them du miles. Integrating from zero to $\bar{u}$ gives the total cost of commuting.

The central planner's problem is to find the land allocation that minimizes equation (7) subject to (1)–(6) and nonnegativity conditions on all the variables. It is possible to express equation (7) and all the constraints as functionals in the single unknown function $L_1(u)$, and to solve the minimization problem with control theory.[2] But it is also possible to solve the planning problem using only elementary algebra, and the simpler technique will be used here.

The key insight is that, because of the linearity of the model, the solution of the planning problem consists of one or the other of two boundary allocations, which will be referred to as the segregated and integrated allocations.

Under the segregated allocation, all the land in the vicinity of the delivery point is devoted to the production of commodity one. Only commodity one is produced as far out as is necessary to produce the required X units. Suppose this requires all the land out to a distance u^* from the delivery point. Then, between u^* and $\bar{u}$, all the land is devoted to the production of commodity two, and of course the available land is just enough to produce the required X units. This allocation can be expressed as

$$\left.\begin{array}{l} L_1(u) = \phi u \\ L_2(u) = 0 \end{array}\right\} 0 \leq u \leq u^*,$$

$$\left.\begin{array}{l} L_1(u) = 0 \\ L_2(u) = \phi u \end{array}\right\} u^* < u \leq \bar{u},$$

$$u^* = \left[\frac{2X}{\phi a_1}\right]^{\frac{1}{2}}.$$

Under the integrated allocation, land at each u is divided between

2. See Arrow [2] for a superb exposition of basic control theory.

production of the two commodities so that $X_1(u) = X_2(u)$, and all the available land is used. Under this allocation,

$$L_1(u) = \frac{a_2\phi u}{a_1 + a_2}$$
$$L_2(u) = \frac{a_1\phi u}{a_1 + a_2}$$
$$0 \leq u \leq \bar{u}.$$

The two allocations are shown graphically in figure 4.

Under the integrated allocation, commodity one is shipped, but workers do not commute, since the number of workers' residences equals the number of jobs at each u. Under the segregated allocation, there is less shipment of commodity one than under the integrated strategy, but there is also some commuting.

It is now possible to establish that only the segregated and integrated allocations can be optimum, and to find the condition under which each will be the solution to the problem. The procedure is to start with a segregated allocation and to ask whether transportation costs can be reduced by partial integration of residences and workplaces. It will be shown that if any integration is desirable then so is the complete adoption of the integrated strategy.

Under the segregated strategy, consider an acre of land located at u', $0 < u' \leq u^*$, on which a_1 units of commodity one are produced. Next, find another acre, located at u'', $u^* < u'' \leq \bar{u}$, on which a_2 units of commodity two are produced. Choose u' and u'' so that all the workers employed on the acre at u' live farther from the city center than u'', and so that all the workers residing on the acre at u'' work closer to the city center than u'. Two such points certainly exist, not just under the segregated allocation, but under any allocation that satisfies (6) as a strict inequality. Write $\Delta u = u'' - u' > 0$ for the distance between the two locations.

Now suppose that the production of the a_1 units of commodity one is moved from u' to u'', and that the production of the a_2 units of commodity

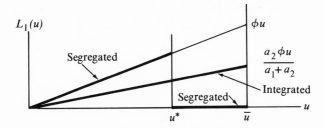

Figure 4. Segregated and Integrated Land Allocations.

two is moved from u'' to u'. The move increases the cost of transporting commodity one by $t_1a_1\Delta u$. But it decreases the cost of commuting by $t_2a_2\Delta u + t_2a_1\Delta u$. The first term results from the fact that the a_2 workers formerly living on the acre at u'' now travel Δu fewer miles to work. The second term results from the fact that the a_1 workers formerly employed on the acre at u' also now travel Δu fewer miles to work. As a result of the trade, total transportation cost changes by

(8) $(t_1a_1 - t_2a_2 - t_2a_1)\Delta u.$

The trade will decrease total transportation cost if and only if the expression is negative, i.e., if and only if

(9) $$\frac{t_1 - t_2}{t_2} < \frac{a_2}{a_1}.$$

Note that the sign of (8) depends only on the sign of Δu and not on its magnitude. Furthermore, values of u' and u'' can be found so that $\Delta u > 0$, provided only the integrated allocation is not in effect. Finally, a trade of the kind under consideration leaves unchanged the total production of commodities one and two and the total land required. It follows that, if (9) holds, trades can be found that will decrease total transportation cost until the integrated allocation is adopted. In other words, if a little integration pays, then complete integration pays. If the inequality is in the opposite direction in (9), then the opposite argument holds. Starting from an integrated allocation, trades can be found that will decrease total transportation costs until the segregated allocation is reached. If (9) holds as an equality, then any allocation satisfying (6) is optimum. Roughly, all allocations between the segregated and integrated incur the same total transportation costs.

We can summarize the solution of the planning problem as follows: if

$$\frac{t_1 - t_2}{t_2} < \frac{a_2}{a_1},$$

then the integrated allocation is optimum; if

$$\frac{t_1 - t_2}{t_2} > \frac{a_1}{a_1},$$

then the segregated allocation is optimum; if

$$\frac{t_1 - t_2}{t_2} = \frac{a_2}{a_1},$$

then all strategies are optimum provided they do not entail outward commuting.

The first of these inequalities will certainly hold if $t_1 < t_2$, i.e., if it is cheaper to transport export goods than commuters. Whether that is so depends on the units in which output is measured, but it should be remembered that the analysis has been carried out in units such that each worker produces one unit of export goods. In these units, $t_1 < t_2$ says that it is cheaper to transport what one worker produces than to transport the worker. In that case, it pays to avoid transporting workers by adopting the integrated allocation. But, even if $t_1 > t_2$, the first inequality will hold if a_2 is sufficiently large in relation to a_1. In this case, even though freight is more expensive than commuting, an acre of land devoted to commodity two is highly productive compared to an acre devoted to commodity one. Then a movement toward the integrated allocation requires more shipment of a few units of commodity one, but less commuting by many workers, and is therefore desirable.

3. Land Allocation by Competitive Markets

In this section, it is assumed that land is allocated by competitive markets rather than by a central planner. The important question is, of course, whether competitive markets will reproduce the efficient allocation of land found in the previous section. The model is a simple one, and it should not be surprising to find that competitive markets are efficient. But it is worthwhile to present the analysis in detail because there are almost no results in the literature concerning the efficiency of spatial competition. The major paper on the subject, Koopmans and Beckmann [14], is pessimistic about the possibility of efficient markets in a spatial context.

Competitive equilibrium must of course satisfy equations (1)–(5) in section 1; i.e., the markets must produce the required amounts of commodities one and two with the available technology. In addition, markets must generate enough revenues to pay for the production of the two commodities, for the required shipment of commodity one, and for the required commuting of workers. Finally, in equilibrium, it must not be profitable to change the location of any activity.

The classic notion of the theory of land rent is, of course, that landowners rent their land to the potential user offering the highest rent. Furthermore, land rent must equate to zero the profit earned by users of land. Then locational equilibrium requires that no potential land user be able to offer more rent than is being paid for any site and still make at least zero profit. In the present model, rent must be zero at the edge of the urban area, since land has no nonurban use. Letting $R(u)$ be the rental per square mile of land at a distance u from the city center, we can therefore write

$$(10) \qquad\qquad\qquad R(\bar{u}) = 0.$$

The obvious alternative assumption, employed in later chapters, is that rent on land used for nonurban purposes is a positive constant. Then $R(\bar{u})$ would be equated to that constant in equation (10), but the market allocation of urban land would be unaffected and only trivial changes would be required in the following analysis.

Since land is the only input in the production of housing services, the housing services are free at $u = \bar{u}$. It is assumed that the required number of workers can be attracted to the urban area if housing is free, there is no commuting, and the wage rate is W. Thus, if there is any production of commodity one at $\bar{u}$, i.e., if $X_1(\bar{u}) > 0$, the wage rate will be $W(\bar{u}) = W$. If the worker lives or works closer to the city center, he must be compensated accordingly. If a worker both lives and works at u, the wage rate must cover the higher cost of housing there, so we must have

$$(11) \qquad\qquad\qquad W(u) = W + p_2(u),$$

where $p_2(u)$ is the price per unit of housing services at u. If, alternatively, the worker is to be induced to commute to u, he must be paid enough to cover the cost of commuting, so

$$(12) \qquad\qquad\qquad W(u) = W + t_2(\bar{u} - u).$$

It is important to note that, if the market is to yield the integrated allocation of land, then it must be cheaper for workers to live where they work than to commute. Comparison between equations (11) and (12) shows that this entails

$$(13) \qquad\qquad\qquad p_2(u) < t_2(\bar{u} - u).$$

The next requirements for market equilibrium are that profits must be just zero wherever commodities one and two are produced. We can write these conditions as

$$(14) \quad \pi_1(u) = p_1(u)X_1(u) - R(u)L_1(u) - W(u)X_1(u) = 0 \text{ if } X_1(u) > 0,$$

$$(15) \qquad \pi_2(u) = p_2(u)X_2(u) - R(u)L_2(u) = 0 \text{ if } X_2(u) > 0.$$

Here, $\pi_i(u)$ is the profit from producing commodity i at a distance u, and $p_1(u)$ is the price at which commodity one can be sold at u. The price at the delivery point must exceed this by the cost of shipping the commodity to the delivery point. The final equilibrium requirement is that producers of commodity one must be able to deliver the commodity at a price no higher than the price at which it can be delivered from other locations, i.e.,

$$(16) \qquad p_1 = p_1(u) + t_1 u \text{ if } X_1(u) > 0,$$

where p_1 is the delivered price of commodity one.

We are now ready to answer the basic question. Will the competitive markets described by the foregoing equations produce the efficient allocation of land that was computed in the previous section? The first step in answering the question is to compute the two product prices and the two factor prices under the integrated and segregated land allocations.

If the market system is to yield the integrated allocation, then not only must equations (1)–(5) and (10) be satisfied, but also (11) and (14)–(16), and $X_1(u) = X_2(u)$ must hold for all values of u between zero and $\bar{u}$. Easy calculations show that these conditions imply

$$(17) \qquad p_1 = t_1\bar{u} + W.$$

$$(18) \qquad R(u) = \frac{t_1 a_1 a_2}{a_1 + a_2}(\bar{u} - u),$$

$$(19) \qquad p_1(u) = W + t_1(\bar{u} - u),$$

$$(20) \qquad p_2(u) = \frac{t_1 a_1}{a_1 + a_2}(\bar{u} - u),$$

$$(21) \qquad W(u) = W + \frac{t_1 a_1}{a_1 + a_2}(\bar{u} - u).$$

Equation (17) says that the delivered price of commodity one is the cost of producing it at the most distant location and shipping it to the delivery point. Equations (18)–(21) show that the two product prices and the two factor prices are linear in distance from the delivery point.

Next, suppose that the market yields the segregated land allocation. In this case, equations (1)–(5) and (10) must be satisfied; (12), (14), and (16) must hold for $0 \leq u \leq u^*$; and (15) must hold for $u^* < u \leq \bar{u}$. These conditions imply

$$(22) \qquad p_1 = W + t_1 u^* + \frac{a_1 + a_2}{a_1} t_2(\bar{u} - u^*),$$

$$(23) \quad R(u) = \begin{cases} t_2 a_2(\bar{u} - u^*) + (t_1 - t_2)a_1(u^* - u), & 0 \leq u \leq u^* \\ t_2 a_2(\bar{u} - u) & u^* < u \leq \bar{u} \end{cases}$$

$$(24) \quad p_1(u) = W + \frac{a_1 + a_2}{a_1} t_2(\bar{u} - u^*) + t_1(u^* - u), \qquad 0 \leq u \leq u^*$$

$$(25) \qquad p_2(u) = t_2(\bar{u} - u), \qquad u^* < u \leq \bar{u}$$

$$(26) \qquad W(u) = W + t_2(\bar{u} - u). \qquad 0 \leq u \leq u^*.$$

It can be seen that $p_1(u)$, $p_2(u)$ and $W(u)$ are again linear in the relevant ranges of u, but $R(u)$ is piecewise linear, with a kink at $u = u^*$.

We have now computed product and factor prices under the two possible optimum allocations of land. The next step is to ask whether anyone would have an incentive to move if markets were allocating land in one of these two ways. If someone has an incentive to move from a given allocation then that allocation cannot be a market solution.

Consider first the segregated allocation in which equations (22)–(26) hold. Either producers of commodity one or workers might have an incentive to move. Suppose a worker tries to move his residence from a u between u^* and $\bar{u}$ to his place of work at a distance u' between zero and u^*. At u' he must pay the land rent indicated by equation (23). Thus, his housing will cost

$$p_2(u') = R(u')/a_2 = t_2(\bar{u} - u^*) + (t_1 - t_2)\frac{a_1}{a_2}(u^* - u').$$

At his old residence, his housing plus commuting costs were, using (25),

$$t_2(\bar{u} - u').$$

The move will be profitable if $p_2(u') < t_2(\bar{u} - u')$. After some manipulation, this inequality reduces to

$$\frac{t_1 - t_2}{t_2} < \frac{a_2}{a_1}.$$

It was shown in the previous section that this is precisely the condition under which the integrated allocation is efficient. Thus, starting from a segregated allocation, the market provides workers with an incentive to move toward an integrated allocation only if the integrated allocation is the efficient one. Now suppose that a producer of commodity one tries to move from a u between zero and u^* to a value u' of u between u^* and $\bar{u}$. In that case, he will have to pay the land rent at u' indicated by equation (23). His profit will be

$$\pi_1(u') = (p_1 - t_1u')X_1(u') - R(u')L_1(u') - W(u')X_1(u').$$

Using equation (26), this expression will be positive if

$$\frac{t_1 - t_2}{t_2} < \frac{a_1}{a_2},$$

which is precisely the condition for the integrated strategy to be efficient. Thus, as was true with workers, producers of commodity one have an incentive to move from the segregated allocation toward an integrated allocation only if the integrated allocation is efficient.

If, instead of starting from a segregated allocation, we start from an integrated allocation we can use exactly the same procedure to investigate whether workers or producers have incentive to move toward a segregated allocation. And the results are exactly the same: markets provide workers and producers with incentive to move toward an integrated allocation under precisely the conditions in which the integrated allocation is efficient.

It has just been shown that markets will provide workers and producers with incentive to move from inefficient and toward efficient allocations. The next step is to show that movement will continue until the efficient allocation is reached. First, if one worker or producer has incentive to move from a segregated or integrated allocation, then all have, because of the linearity of the model. Second, no intermediate allocation (in which there are some residing at a given u and some commuting to the same u) can be an equilibrium allocation. If workers live and work at u, then equation (11) must hold. If they also commute to u, (12) must hold. Together, (11) and (12) imply $p_2(u) = t_2(\bar{u} - u)$. Then, the zero profit condition for housing services, (15), implies $R(u) = t_2 a_2(\bar{u} - u)$. But the zero profit condition for commodity one, (14), implies

$$R(u) = (p_1 - W - t_2 a_1 \bar{u}) - (t_1 - t_2)a_1 u.$$

These two equations for $R(u)$ are consistent only if $(t_1 - t_2)a_1 = t_2 a_2$, which is the condition for all allocations to be efficient.

The final step is the observation that the delivered price of commodity one is always lower if the efficient allocation is used: p_1 computed from (22) is less than p_1 computed from (17) if and only if the segregated allocation is efficient.

We can summarize as follows: Only the segregated and integrated allocations can satisfy all the conditions for market equilibrium. If one of these allocations is efficient and we start from the other one, markets provide workers and producers with incentive to move toward the efficient allocation. Only when the efficient allocation is achieved will all the equilibrium conditions be satisfied and no worker or producer have incentive to move. It can thus be concluded that competitive markets will produce and sustain an efficient allocation of land in the model studied in this chapter.

4. SOME NUMERICAL VALUES

The model analyzed in this chapter is far too unrealistic to justify serious empirical estimation and testing. Intra-urban area variation in factor proportions, especially in the capital-land ratio, is one of the most dramatic urban phenomena, and it is excluded from the model. Also, the level of aggregation is high, and there is no demand side.

Nevertheless, it may be worthwhile to establish the roughest orders of magnitude for the relevant parameters. Such calculations should provide an idea of the likelihood that the segregated or integrated allocation might be efficient. And the very simplicity of the model makes it possible to calculate relevant parameters at least roughly from readily available data. The interesting calculation is, of course, to find the direction of the inequality that was shown in section 2 to determine which allocation is optimum.

It is easy to calculate rough orders of magnitude for t_1 and t_2. Those that follow pertain to the mid-1960s. Data presented by Friedlaender [10, p. 39] suggest that a typical ton of freight has a value between $500 and $2,000, and that the ton-mile cost of freight shipment is between $0.25 and $0.75. Value added per worker per day is about $40. These data suggest that the average worker produces between 0.02 and 0.08 tons of output per day. Then the freight cost of shipping a worker's daily output one mile would be between $0.005[= ($0.25)(0.02)] and $0.06[= ($0.75)(0.08)]. Thus t_1 is probably in the range $0.005 \leq t_1 \leq$ $0.06. The endpoints of the range differ by a factor of twelve.

There is much less uncertainty about t_2. Operating costs per passenger-mile of cars and transit vehicles are usually between $0.05 and $0.10 (see Meyer, Kain, and Wohl [18]). If, as a guess, travel time is valued at between $2.00 and $4.00, and commuting travel speed is assumed to be 20 miles per hour, commuting cost per mile is between $0.15 and $0.30. These figures must be doubled since workers must make a round trip each day. The result is $0.30 \leq t_2 \leq$ $0.60.

The lower end of the range for t_2 is five times the upper end of the range for t_1. Unless the figures are very far out of line, it must be concluded that $t_2 > t_1$. Indeed, it is not surprising to find that the cost of commuting two miles for the average United States worker exceeds the cost of shipping what he produces one mile.

These calculations suggest that integrated production should be more profitable and more efficient than segregated production in United States conditions in the mid-1960s. But the implications should not be pushed too far. At most, they are relevant only to the production of goods that are shipped outside the urban area. Of the employment sectors studied in chapter 3, only manufacturing comes close to satisfying the conditions of the model in this chapter. Undoubtedly, a major reason for the suburbanization of manufacturing in recent decades has been the rapid increase in the use of roads to export manufactured goods from urban areas, thus avoiding the shipment of goods through congested city centers to harbors and railheads. But the calculations in this section suggest that convergence of population and manufacturing employment density functions might have occurred, at least to a considerable extent, even if most manufactured goods still had to be shipped to city centers for export.

5. CONCLUSION

The model analyzed in this chapter is unrealistic in many ways, some of which will be eliminated in the more complicated models in later chapters. The most important modification is to introduce factor substitution. Factor proportions vary enormously both within and among urban areas. The capital-land ratio, for example, may vary by a factor of 100 within ten or twenty miles in a large metropolitan area. The second important modification is the introduction of a demand side for both locally consumed and exported goods. Third, a more elaborate representation of the urban transportation system is needed. Other steps toward realism, not taken in this book, would be the introduction of several labor inputs representing different skill levels, introduction of intermediate goods, and introduction of a public sector.

Unfortunately, the introduction of even apparently minor complications makes it difficult to determine whether competitive markets allocate land and other resources efficiently. It seems unlikely that the introduction of factor substitution would deprive markets of their efficiency. But the introduction of a demand side means that demand per capita will vary from place to place in the urban area, since prices will vary. This is a fundamental modification which makes the efficiency of markets very hard to establish. Likewise, a transportation system that competes with other sectors for land and other factors of production greatly complicates the analysis and necessitates the resort to numerical analysis of the model. Much more work is needed on the efficiency of spatial competition.

6

A Complex Model with Congestion

The previous chapter contained an analysis of the simplest model in which interesting questions can be posed about the locations of related economic activities in an urban area. At the end of the chapter, several possible generalizations of the model were suggested. Some of those generalizations are incorporated in the model presented in this chapter and analyzed in the next chapter. Some possible further generalizations are discussed in chapter 9.

The focus in this and the next chapter is on the relationship among the kinds, amounts, and locations of housing and the costs of commuting. A major purpose of the analysis is to use a theoretical general equilibrium model to gain insight into the causes of the historical flattening of population density functions that were recorded in chapter 3. We want to ask, for example: What are the directions and magnitudes of the effects on population density of changes in income, commuting costs, and the total population of the urban area? Among the historical phenomena recorded in chapters 2 and 3 some, unfortunately, cannot be analyzed with the model in this chapter. By far the most important such phenomenon is the historical flattening of employment density functions. The difficulties encountered in attempts to make the location of employment endogenous in the model are discussed in chapter 9.

The model presented here has of course benefited from many of the models surveyed in chapter 4. Like any model of land allocation by market processes, it builds on the work of Alonso [1]. But it bears the greatest resemblance to the work of Muth [26]. A major difference between this model and Muth's is that this one has an articulated transportation system, including a representation of the causes and effects of congestion. The major elements in the model are discussed briefly in this section.

Suppose that an exogenously determined number of people works in the central business district. Workers live in the area surrounding the

CBD and commute to the CBD. Population density will be high in the residential area and the residential area will be correspondingly small if the amount of housing per worker is small or if housing services are provided with a high ratio of capital to land inputs. The capital-land ratio will be high if housing services are provided by multistory dwellings or if dwellings are on properties that include little uncovered land around the building. Population density will fall with distance from the city center if land is substituted for capital in the production of housing services at locations distant from the CBD. The foregoing indicates that the population density function will depend on the characteristics of the production and demand functions for housing services, and on prices of inputs and outputs in the market for housing services.

Housing demand and the population density function are also related to commuting costs and conditions. Each worker must make one round trip each work day between his home and the CBD. Thus in this model commuting is entirely determined by residential location. The number of commuters that must pass through a given distance, say five miles, from the CBD, is the number of workers who live at least that far from the CBD. Thus, the more decentralized the urban area, i.e., the flatter the population density function, the more commuting there will be at each distance from the CBD. The amount of commuting is less dependent on the shape of the population density function the closer one gets to the edge of the CBD. In this model, no one lives in the CBD. Thus all workers must commute across the edge of the CBD regardless of the population density function. Workers are in locational equilibrium with respect to their residences if the savings in housing costs resulting from a move farther out are just offset by increased commuting costs.

In this chapter, the attempt is to represent commuting costs realistically as they exist in most United States metropolitan areas where commuting is dominated by the automobile. The capacity of the transportation system is determined by the resources devoted to it, and they are exogenous to the model. The cost per commuter mile depends on the use made of the system: congestion slows travel time and therefore increases commuting costs. The major complications in the model result from the interaction between housing location and commuting decisions. The more workers that live beyond a certain distance from the CBD, the greater the commuting at that distance and the greater the commuting cost per mile. If commuting costs are high, workers demand either little housing or capital-intensive housing, both of which economize on commuting.

The work of Walters [34], Mohring and Harwitz [24], and others indicates that a transportation system of the kind just described leads to an inefficient use of transportation resources. Each worker makes his location and commuting decisions on the basis of his commuting (and housing) costs. Each worker's commuting cost per mile is the same at a given distance from the CBD and is therefore equal to the average cost per commuter mile at that distance. But travel cost per commuter increases with the number of commuters (at least if there are enough commuters) because of congestion. Since marginal cost must exceed the average if the average cost is rising, the increase in travel cost to all commuters exceeds the average cost per commuter, which is paid by each additional commuter. Streets are therefore characterized by average cost pricing and the result is inefficient and excessive use of transportation facilities. In chapter 8, the assumptions concerning the transportation system are altered somewhat, so that commuting decisions conform to the usual marginal efficiency conditions of welfare economics. It is then possible to examine the effect of efficient transportation pricing on the locational structure of the urban area.

Specific assumptions for the model analyzed in this and the following chapter are made in the next section.

1. THE MODEL

The urban area considered in this model has a well defined CBD, whose location and size are given from outside the model. The urban area might exist for any of the reasons discussed in chapter 1. It might, for example, be at a port, or there might be scale economies in a key industry or set of industries. The CBD consists of all or part of a circle with radius ϵ, and the model contains no analysis of what happens inside the CBD. It is assumed that the urban area's labor force of N workers is exogenous and entirely employed in the CBD.

Outside the CBD, land is used for workers' residences and for commuting. It is assumed that land is available for urban uses in all directions from the CBD except for a pie slice of $2\pi - \phi$ radians. In this situation, urban development will occur uniformly around the ϕ radians, since land rents and population density will depend only on distance and not on direction from the CBD. It is assumed that land is available for urban uses as far away from the CBD as is necessary to satisfy the equilibrium conditions developed below. All land outside the CBD has an alternative to urban use, e.g., in agriculture. The land rent in the alternative use is an exogenous amount R_A per acre or square mile. The urban area stops at the distance u_A from the center of the CBD at which urban residents can offer no more than R_A for the land, and they are therefore unable to bid land beyond u_A away from agricultural users. The model will, of course, determine u_A.

Housing services are produced with capital and land inputs, and input and output markets are competitive. The rental rate on capital is exogenous, assumed to be established on a national market of which the urban area is only a small part. The rental rate on capital is the same at all locations in the urban area. The rental rate on land is the same to all customers at a given distance from the city center, but it is endogenous and may vary with distance from the center. The function giving land rent at each distance from the center is the key function to be determined by the model. Rental rates on capital and land are the same to all owners of these inputs (at a given distance from the center, in the case of land), and therefore the distinction between owners and renters of houses vanishes.

A strong assumption in the model is that housing services are produced with a Cobb-Douglas production function with constant returns to scale. Following the notation of chapter 5, the output of housing services at a distance u can be written

$$(1) \qquad X_{2S}(u) = A_2 L_2(u)^{\alpha_2} K_2(u)^{1-\alpha_2},$$

where $X_{2S}(u)$ is the supply of housing services and $L_2(u)$ and $K_2(u)$ are inputs of land and capital in the production of housing services at u. The assumptions that there are constant returns to scale, that land rent is the same at all points u miles from the center, and that the rental rate on capital is the same everywhere imply that there is no loss of generality in relating total inputs and total output at u rather than relating inputs and output at each point.

Economists have devoted relatively little effort to the study of capital-land substitution in the production of housing services. "Engineering" production functions have been studied in a variety of physical and chemical processes, many of which are more complex than structures. Aside from variation in the amount of uncovered land surrounding the structure, only two characteristics of multistory buildings seem relevant. First, the more floors there are, the more capital must be used on lower floors to support the upper floors. Second, the more floors there are, the larger the space on each that must be devoted to vertical transportation. Certainly, the capital-land ratio varies enormously between downtown and suburb. A detached suburban home on a one-acre plot may have a capital-land ratio of eight (rooms) per acre. A downtown highrise of only modest height may easily have ten times the capital-land ratio of the suburban home. Of course (as follows from equations (2) and (3) below), the ratio of inputs is proportional to the ratio of input prices if the production function is Cobb-Douglas and input markets are competitive. If, as is approximately true, capital costs are the same downtown and in the suburbs, then a ten-to-one variation in the capital-land ratio should be associated with a ten-to-one variation in land values between downtown and suburb. For example, suburban land might be valued at \$10,000 per acre and downtown land at \$100,000 per acre. Casual empiricism suggests that factor proportions vary less than relative factor prices between downtown and suburb. If this is so, it indicates an elasticity of substitution less than the unitary value implied by the Cobb-Douglas production function. It seems plausible, but definite results must await further study. In any case, the present model becomes extremely complicated if another production function, such as the constant elasticity of substitution (CES), is substituted for the Cobb-Douglas.

Equilibrium in input markets requires that the value of the marginal product equal the input price for each input,

$$(2) \qquad\qquad \frac{\alpha_2 p_2(u) X_{2S}(u)}{L_2(u)} = R(u),$$

$$(3) \qquad\qquad \frac{(1 - \alpha_2) p_2(u) X_{2S}(u)}{K_2(u)} = r.$$

Here, $p_2(u)$ is the price of housing services and $R(u)$ and r are the rental rates of land and capital; $R(u)$ is endogenous and r is exogenous.

The demand for housing services per family living u miles from the center is

$$(4) \qquad\qquad x_{2D}(u) = B_2 p_2(u)^{\theta_2} W^{\theta_1}.$$

Here, $x_{2D}(u)$ is the housing-services demand per worker at u and W is income per worker; θ_1 and θ_2 are the income and own-price elasticities of demand for housing services. Equation (4), being analogous to the Cobb-Douglas production function (1), is justified by its mathematical and computational convenience. Like the Cobb-Douglas, it is, of course, frequently used in empirical work. It has been extensively used in studies of the demand for housing services by Reid [31], and by Muth [26], and a good deal is known about values of the two demand elasticities. W is exogenous to the model, but it is included in (4) because considerable interest centers on the effect of increases in income on suburbanization in urban areas. It should be noted that the cost of commuting does not appear in (4). Attempts to include it made the model impossibly cumbersome. As will be shown below, commuting costs do have an indirect effect on housing demand.

Total housing service demand at u is housing service demand per worker multiplied by the number of workers living at u,

$$(5) \qquad\qquad X_{2D}(u) = x_{2D}(u) N(u),$$

where $X_{2D}(u)$ is total demand for housing services at u and $N(u)$ is the number of workers living u miles from the center. Equilibrium in the market for housing services also requires that supply equal demand at each u,

$$(6) \qquad\qquad X_{2D}(u) = X_{2S}(u).$$

The key equation related to housing services is the one that defines locational equilibrium. Some restriction is needed in the market to ensure that the equilibrium distribution of residential locations is one from which no one has incentive to move. Several such restrictions were discussed in the survey in chapter 4. The one employed here states that, if a worker living u miles from the city center demands the housing services indicated by equation (4), then the change in the cost of these housing services resulting from any move toward or away from the city center will be just offset by the change in commuting costs. This condition can be written

$$(7) \qquad\qquad x_{2D}(u)p_2'(u) + p_3(u) = 0.$$

Here $p_3(u)$ is two times commuting cost per mile at u. Cost per mile is multiplied by two because a move one mile farther away from the center requires two extra miles of commuting, one mile toward the center in the morning and one mile away from the center in the evening. The term $p_3(u)$ is endogenous, while $p_2'(u)$ is the derivative of $p_2(u)$ with respect to u.

The transportation system in the model is easiest to interpret if it is thought of as a system of radial roads or highways. It might be possible to think of it as a bus or subway system, but the interpretation would be more strained. Suppose the public sector lays out a road system and that the system's design capacity at each u is proportionate to the land devoted to transportation at that u—specifically,

$$(8) \qquad\qquad X_{3S}(u) = A_3 L_3(u),$$

where $L_3(u)$ is the amount of land devoted to transportation at a distance u miles from the center, and $X_{3S}(u)$ is the resulting design capacity of the transportation system at that distance. Equation (8) is obviously a special case of the Cobb-Douglas production function in which the exponent of capital is zero. The model would not be much more complicated if (8) were written analogously to (1), and the exogenously determined supply $X_{3S}(u)$ were assumed to be produced with the cost minimizing combination of capital and land. But it would add little to the realism of the model, and the simpler form in (8) is retained. Then it is a matter of indifference whether $X_{3S}(u)$ or $L_3(u)$ is assumed to be the exogenous variable.

The demand side of the transportation system is more complex. It is assumed that workers use the transportation system to the extent that costs make it in their interest to do so. Each worker makes one trip each way daily between his home and the CBD, and the use of the transportation system is therefore entirely determined by the locations of residences. Transportation demand at u equals the number of workers who live beyond u,

$$(9) \qquad X_{3D}(u) = N - \int_{\epsilon}^{u} N(u')du',$$

where $X_{3D}(u)$ is transportation demand at a distance u from the center. A basic characteristic of any urban transportation system is that use of it by commuters may exceed its design capacity. In a bus or subway system, commuters must wait in long queues, and travel times are long because of congested rights-of-way and because of longer and more frequent stops. In a road or highway system, the right-of-way becomes congested and travel times increase. Considerable research has been undertaken in recent years concerning the relationship between the use made of a road or highway and the travel speed on it. Important references are Mohring and Harwitz [24] and Walters [34]. The basic idea is, of course, that travel speed decreases as the number of users increases. Reduced speed increases the time and, to a small extent, the operating cost of travel. Several different formulas have been suggested to represent the relationship between travel cost, number of users, and design capacity of the road. The one used here is a variant of that suggested by Vickery [33],

$$(10) \qquad p_3(u) = \bar{p}_3 + \rho_1 \left[\frac{X_{3D}(u)}{X_{3S}(u)} \right]^{\rho_2}.$$

Here $\bar{p}_3$ is two times the sum of operating and time cost per commuter-mile in the absence of congestion. On a public transit vehicle it represents the fare plus the time cost of uncongested travel. In a car it represents the cost of operating the vehicle plus the time cost of uncongested travel. Included in $\bar{p}_3$ is any fuel tax levied by the public sector to pay for the capital and land costs of the transportation system.

The second term on the right of equation (10) represents congestion cost. It assumes that congestion cost per commuter at u is proportionate to a power of the ratio of $X_{3D}(u)$ to $X_{3S}(u)$. Vickery believes that ρ_2 is at least two. This would mean that a doubling of the number of commuters at u would quadruple congestion costs per commuter at u. Evidence presented by writers referred to above suggests that congestion costs rise rapidly as road use increases in relation to design capacity. Thus, as in actual urban transportation systems, nothing in the model ensures that transportation demand will be limited to design capacity of the system. Of course, the extent to which the model produces a locational pattern that avoids congestion is a key property of the system to be investigated. Equation (1) assumes that some congestion occurs even at very low usage of the street or highway. Some formulas assume that travel cost is a constant until usage exceeds design capacity. In that case, equation (10) must be considered an approximation.

An important simplification of reality has been made here and is retained throughout the following chapters. It is that the only relevant dimension of the urban transportation system is radial distance to the city center. There is no crosstown travel to places of work since all employment is in the CBD, and the assumptions ignore any crosstown travel to gain access to radial transportation routes. Any more complex and realistic assumptions require that all locations be specified by two dimensions, distance and direction, which would greatly complicate the model.

The last equation that must hold for each u ensures that all the land available at each u within the urban area and outside the CBD will be used either for housing or for transportation. Within a small interval du miles wide centered on a distance u miles from the center, $L_2(u)du$ square miles are used for housing and $L_3(u)du$ square miles for transportation. Since a pie slice of $2\pi - \phi$ radians is unavailable for urban use, the total available land in the interval is $\phi u du$. Therefore, we must have

$$(11) \qquad L_2(u) + L_3(u) = \phi u.$$

Equations (1)–(11) must hold for each value of u in the interval $\epsilon \leq u \leq u_A$.

The model is completed by two equations that relate to the overall equilibrium of the urban area. First, land is used for urban purposes only if it can be bid away from agricultural users. Therefore, the edge of the urban area will be u_A miles away from the city center where u_A satisfies

$$(12) \qquad R(u_A) = R_A.$$

R_A is exogenous, but u_A is endogenous. Second, all the workers employed in the CBD must be housed somewhere in the urban area, so we must have

$$(13) \qquad \int_\epsilon^{u_A} N(u)du = N,$$

where N is the exogenously determined labor force.

Equations (1)–(13) complete the model. An economically meaningful solution of the system must include only nonnegative values of all the variables. Most economists would probably agree that the model contains only elementary economic concepts. Nevertheless, it is mathematically cumbersome. Its solution consists of eleven unknown functions of u [$X_{2D}(u)$, $X_{2S}(u)$, $L_2(u)$, $x_{2D}(u)$, $p_2(u)$, $R(u)$, $K_2(u)$, $N(u)$, $p_3(u)$, $X_{3S}(u)$, and $X_{3D}(u)$] and the value of one variable (u_A). Equations (1)–(11) are eleven simultaneous equations relating the eleven unknown functions at each u. One of these equations, (7), is a differential equation. Between them, (12) and (13) provide a solution for the unknown variable u_A and an initial condition for the solution of the differential equation. The solution of the model is discussed in the next section.

2. SOLUTION

Mathematical systems as complex as the one in section 1 usually do not yield solutions in which the functions can be written explicitly in terms of u. The solution must consist of the derivation of a more or less complete set of characteristics of the eleven functions. Some of these characteristics are easy to derive. For example, equation (7) implies that $p_2'(u) < 0$ and $p_2(u)$ is therefore a decreasing function of u. Furthermore, it follows from (15) below that $p_2'(u)$ and $R'(u)$ have the same signs. Thus, both land rent and the price of housing services decrease with distance from the city center. But the set of characteristics that can be derived mathematically is small and incomplete. One would like to know how sensitive land rents, housing costs, and population density are to changes in the system's parameters. One would like to know in detail the shape of the land rent, population density, and transportation cost functions. One would like to know how much traffic congestion the system produces and how congestion varies as income increases or transportation technology improves. It has been possible to answer almost none of these questions using mathematical analysis. It was therefore decided to study the properties of the model using numerical analysis and with the help of a computer. The design of the numerical computations and their results are presented in the next chapter. The remainder of this section shows the manipulations that were performed on the model to prepare a set of instructions with which the computer could solve the model. Readers not interested in these details may skip the remainder of this chapter.

Since a great deal is known about numerical solutions of differential equations, the obvious procedure seems to be to find a set of substitutions that will express the differential equation (7) in terms of a single unknown function of u and its derivative. Both economic intuition and extensive manipulation of the model suggest that the land rent function $R(u)$ is the key function in the model. Once it has been computed, most of the other interesting functions can be computed either with simple computer programs or with a desk calculator. The procedure for computing $R(u)$ that is described in the following paragraphs was worked out by trial and error, taking advantage of several special features of the model.

Substituting equations (8) and (9) for the supply and demand for transportation in (10), and then substituting the result for $p_3(u)$ in (7), we get

$$(14) \qquad x_{2D}(u)p_2'(u) + \bar{p}_3 + \rho_1\left[\frac{N - \int_\epsilon^u N(u')du'}{A_3L_3(u)}\right]^{p_2} = 0.$$

It is well known that the Cobb-Douglas production function (1) and the factor market equilibrium conditions (2) and (3) imply

$$(15) \qquad p_2(u) = [A_2\alpha_2^{\alpha_2}(1 - \alpha_2)^{1-\alpha_2}]^{-1}r^{1-\alpha_2}R(u)^{\alpha_2} = CR(u)^{\alpha_2},$$

where

$$C = [A_2\alpha_2^{\alpha_2}(1 - \alpha_2)^{1-\alpha_2}]^{-1}r^{1-\alpha_2},$$

thus,

$$(16) \qquad p_2'(u) = \alpha_2 CR(u)^{\alpha_2-1}R'(u).$$

Equations (15) and (16) express $p_2(u)$ and $p_2'(u)$ in terms of $R(u)$ and $R'(u)$.

The next step is to express $N(u)$ in terms of $R(u)$. If we use (2) and (3), we can express the supply of housing, $X_{2S}(u)$, in (1) as

$$(17) \qquad X_{2S}(u) = A_2\left(\frac{1 - \alpha_2}{\alpha_2 r}\right)^{1-\alpha_2}R(u)^{1-\alpha_2}L_2(u).$$

Now (17) can be substituted for $X_{2S}(u)$ in (6). Then, substituting (15) in (4), (4) in (5), and the result in (6), and rearranging terms, we get

$$(18) \qquad N(u) = G^{-1}L_2(u)R(u)^{-\alpha},$$

where

$$G = A_2^{-1}\left(\frac{1 - \alpha_2}{\alpha_2 r}\right)^{-(1-\alpha_2)}B_2C^{\theta_2}W^{\theta_1},$$

and

$$\alpha = \alpha_2(1 + \theta_2) - 1.$$

Now solve (11) for $L_2(u)$ and substitute in (18), giving

$$(19) \qquad N(u) = G^{-1}[\phi u - L_3(u)]R(u)^{-\alpha}.$$

Now substitute (15) into (4) and the result for $x_{2D}(u)$ in (14), (16) for $p_2'(u)$ in (14), and (19) for $N(u)$ in (14). The result is

$$(20) \quad DR(u)^\alpha R'(u) + \bar{p}_3 + \rho_1\left[\frac{N - \int_\epsilon^u G^{-1}[\phi u' - L_3(u')]R(u')^{-\alpha}du'}{A_3L_3(u)}\right]^{p_2} = 0,$$

where

$$D = B_2C^{1+\theta_2}W^{\theta_1}\alpha_2.$$

Equation (20) now contains only $R(u)$ among the eleven unknown functions in the model. It also contains the derivative of $R(u)$ and the integral of a function of $R(u)$ and of u. To the best of my knowledge, (20) has no explicit solution in terms of known functions. In deriving (20), all the equations (1)–(11) have been used. Therefore any values of $R(u)$ that satisfy (20) will also satisfy (1)–(11). The computational problem can now be stated as follows:

Find a set of values $R(u)$ that satisfies equation (20) for $\epsilon \leq u \leq u_A$ so that (12) and (13) are satisfied at some value u_A of u.

The basic procedure is to start at one end of the interval $\epsilon \leq u \leq u_A$ and to compute $R(u)$ from (20) at successive values of u until the other end of the interval is reached. It would be possible to start at either end. If one starts at the outer edge of the urban area, $u = u_A$, then the "initial" condition $R(u_A)$ is known from (12), but the value of u_A has to be guessed and the guess verified at the end of the computation when it can be tested whether (13) holds. It should be noted that (13) is satisfied if and only if the numerator in the square bracket of (20) is zero for $u = u_A$. In the computations reported in the next chapter it was decided to start at the edge of the CBD, i.e., at $u = \epsilon$. Then, it is necessary to guess the value $R(\epsilon)$ and to compute (20) at successive values of u until a u is reached that satisfies (12). At that point, (13) is checked. If it does not hold, then a different guess is made of $R(\epsilon)$ and the procedure is repeated.

There are several standard methods of numerical computation that can be used to evaluate an equation like (20).[1] The method used in the computations reported in the next chapter is among the simplest. It involved approximation of $R(u)$ over short intervals by a linear function. Suppose that by some method we have computed values $R(i)$ and $R'(i)$ for a value i of u. For values of u between i and a slightly larger number we approximate $R(u)$ by

(21) $$R(u) = a_i + b_i u,$$

where

$$a_i = R(i) - iR'(i),$$
$$b_i = R'(i).$$

Using the approximation (21) for $R(u)$, $R'(u)$ can be computed from (20) for a value of u slightly larger than i. For the same value of u, $R(u)$ is computed from (21). Then the procedure is repeated, using a new approximation, for another small interval of u.

---

1. See, for example, Scarborough [32].

If the true function $R(u)$ is smooth, then the approximation can be made as accurate as is desired by using sufficiently small intervals of u. In the application considered here, $R(u)$ is steep for small values of u and becomes flatter as u increases. Thus, $R'(u)$ is actually increasing at each u, whereas it is assumed constant within small intervals in the approximation. It follows that, for a given $R(\epsilon)$, the computed $R(u)$ will be below the true $R(u)$ for every u greater than ϵ. It is therefore important to use small intervals so that the error remains small. In the computations reported in the next chapter, parameters were chosen so that the computed u_A is about 10 miles. The computations were performed using an interval of 0.1 mile, so that the radius of the urban area is divided into about 100 intervals of equal length. It is believed that the resulting computational errors are small.

The steps written into the computer program[2] are as follows:

(i) Guess $R(\epsilon)$

(ii) Putting $u = \epsilon$ in (20), we get

$$DR(\epsilon)^\alpha R'(\epsilon) + \bar{p}_3 + \rho_1 \left[\frac{N}{A_3 L_3} \right]^{\rho_2} = 0.$$

Using the guess made of $R(\epsilon)$ in step (i), compute $R'(\epsilon)$ from this equation.

(iii) Steps (i) and (ii) yield estimates of $R(u)$ and $R'(u)$ for an initial value $u = \epsilon$. At any value i of u, and starting with $i = \epsilon$, compute $R(i + 0.1)$ from equation (21) and $R'(i + 0.1)$ from (20). (The integrals in equation (20) are evaluated in stepwise fashion, using the linear approximation computed for $R(u)$ for each interval between ϵ and $i + 0.1$.)

(iv) At each value $i + 0.1$, check

(a) Is $R(i + 0.1)$ greater than R_A?

(b) Is the numerator inside the square bracket of equation (20) positive?

(v) If the answers to steps (iv.a) and (iv.b) are positive, go back to step (iii) and repeat for the next interval.

(vi) If the answer to step (iv.a) is negative, but that to (iv.b) is positive, go back to step (i) and raise the guess of $R(\epsilon)$.

---

2. The computations were performed by the real-time–sharing service of the Call-a-Computer Corporation. The program is in Fortran IV and is available on request, at cost. Each iteration requires about 15 seconds. The number of iterations required depends on the accuracy which is desired for the estimate of u_A and on the accuracy of the initial guess of $R(\epsilon)$.

(vii) If the answer to step (iv.a) is positive, but that to (iv.b) is negative, go back to (i) and lower the guess of $R(\epsilon)$.

(viii) If the answers to both (iv.a) and (iv.b) are negative, stop; i is the desired value of u_A.

The justification for the instructions in steps (v)–(viii) is as follows: u_A must be a value of u that satisfies both equations (12) and (13). Suppose a guess of $R(\epsilon)$ leads to the situation described in step (vi). This means that equation (12) holds for some u between i and $i + 0.1$, but that

$$\int_{\epsilon}^{i+0.1} N(u)du < N.$$

Thus, the estimated land rent function has fallen to R_A before the urban area is big enough to hold all the workers. Raising the guess of $R(\epsilon)$ will then have two effects. First, it will increase the value of u at which equation (12) will hold, thus providing more land on which to put workers' residences. Second, it will increase population density at each u, because land has become more expensive. If the guess at $R(\epsilon)$ leads to the situation described in step (vii), the opposite is true; the urban area is big enough to contain all the workers' homes at a value of u such that $R(u) > R_A$. In this case, the guess of $R(\epsilon)$ is too high, and must be lowered. If step (viii) materializes, then u_A lies between i and $i + 0.1$. In the computations reported in the next chapter, the guess of $R(\epsilon)$ was altered manually, by an amount that depended on the amounts by which equations (12) and (13) failed to hold. After some experience with the program was gained, the value of u_A was found after only a few iterations.

7

Numerical Analysis of the Complex Model

The purpose of this chapter is to study the properties of the model presented in chapter 6, using the computational procedure outlined in section 2 of that chapter. There are three basic steps in the analysis: first, choose realistic values for the parameters of the model; second, solve the model and ascertain that it produces an urban area with realistic properties; and third, vary the parameters to ascertain the direction and magnitude of the effects on the endogenous variables of the model. The third step is, of course, the heart of the analysis. It is that step that provides insight into the interesting issues such as the effect of congestion and the causes of decentralization.

Nothing in the model indicates the size of urban area to which it can most accurately be applied. The ideal procedure would be to choose several parameter sets relevant to urban areas of several sizes. But the time and resources required for the analysis precluded thorough study of more than one urban area. It was decided that the most interesting urban area to study would be one of medium size, with a labor force of about 300,000 or a population of about one million. Very small cities lack the interest and diversity to justify study. And very large cities are likely to have locational patterns that are strongly influenced by subcenters away from the city center, as was discussed in chapter 1. Of course, there is no guarantee that the model can produce a realistic city of any size, but an urban area of about a million population seems to give the model as good a chance as is possible.

1. Parameters

There are fifteen parameters and one exogenous function of u to be chosen for the model. No detailed statistical studies were undertaken to estimate the parameters, but a serious attempt was made to obtain the best estimates available for most of them. For the purpose of assigning numerical values, the parameters can be placed in three groups. Some parameters, such as the exponents in the production and demand functions for housing services, have been estimated by others, and their estimates can be used. A second group, containing N and ϵ, is specified immediately once the size and basic characteristics of the urban area are chosen. A third group, consisting of some scale parameters, was chosen experimentally to obtain the most realistic urban area the model could produce, consistent with parameter values assigned by the first two methods.

Units must of course be specified before parameter values can be chosen. Distances, such as values of u, are measured in miles, and areas are therefore measured in square miles. Market values of input and output flows are measured in dollars per day. Parameters whose values vary through time, such as income, were chosen to be roughly representative of conditions in the United States in the mid-1960s.

A detailed description follows of the way each parameter value was chosen:

• α_2 (elasticity of housing service production with respect to land input): $1 - \alpha_2$ is the elasticity of housing service output with respect to capital input. In this model, α_2 and $1 - \alpha_2$ are also equal respectively to the shares of land and capital in revenues from the sale of housing services. Various sources of data[1] suggest that site values typically range from about 10 percent to about 25 percent of total residential property values. Capital and land are, of course, not the only inputs in the production of housing services. Current inputs, such as labor, are also used. But current inputs do not appear in the model, and the shares of capital and land must exhaust total product in producing housing services. Thus, α_2 should be between 0.10 and 0.25, and a value of 0.20 was chosen for this study.

• r (daily rate of return per dollar's worth of capital used in the production of housing services): An annual rate of return of 10 percent was assumed to be representative in residential real estate. This was adjusted to a return per working day to make it comparable with the income parameter w, and a work year was assumed to consist of 240 work days. The daily rate of return is between 0.0004 and 0.0005, and was rounded off to 0.0005.

• w (income per worker per day): Average gross weekly earnings were about $95 in 1965 in the private nonagricultural sector; assuming that earnings are about 75 percent of total income, an average income per day would be about $25.

1. See, for example, the annual reports of the Housing and Home Finance Agency.

• θ_1 (income elasticity of demand for housing): Reid [31] estimated income elasticities of demand for housing that averaged about 1.50, and that value has been used in the present study.

• θ_2 (own price elasticity of demand for housing): Muth [26] has estimated that the price elasticity of demand for housing is about minus one. As was pointed out in chapter 4, this value is an important element in his derivation of the exponential population density function. In Muth's model a price elasticity of minus one yields the exponential population density function. Although an elasticity of minus one does not yield the exponential density function in the present model, some experimentation indicated that the behavior of the differential equation for $R(u)$, equation (20) of chapter 6, is unstable for price elasticities in the vicinity of minus one. The reason is related to the fact that α, which appears as an exponent in several places in that equation, is minus one if θ_2 is minus one, regardless of the values of other parameters. A larger absolute value of θ_2 was therefore wanted, and -1.50 was chosen.

• R_A (daily rent per square mile of land used for nonurban purposes): This figure represents the rent that urban activities must offer to attract land away from agricultural or other nonurban uses. For this study it was assumed that land at the edge of a medium-sized urban area was worth about $3,000 per acre in the mid-1960s, or about $1.9 million per square mile. If it is assumed that land rents are capitalized at 10 percent per year and that, as above, there are 240 work days per year, then the rent per work day of a square mile of agricultural land is about $800.

• N (total labor force in the urban area, or employment in the CBD): The intention was to represent an urban area of about one million people. The labor force is about one-third of the population in the United States, and N was assigned the value 300,000.

• ϕ (number of radians around a circle centered on the center of the CBD that are available for urban use): Since a circle has $2\pi \simeq 6.28$ radians, we must have $0 < \phi \leq 6.28$. For the purpose of this study, ϕ was taken to be 6.28, which means that the urban area will be circular.

• ϵ (radius of the CBD): The assumption that all the urban area's employment is in the CBD is contrary to fact. Hence, there is a certain arbitrariness in the size assumed for the CBD. For the purpose of this study, ϵ was assigned a value of one, which implies a CBD of 3.14 square miles.

• A_2 (scale parameter in the production function for housing services): The value of this parameter depends on the units in which the output of housing services is measured. In this model, A_2 was chosen experimentally so that, with the values assigned to other parameters, it produced a value of u_A and the implied population density that are typical of medium-sized urban areas in the United States. In 1960, the average population density of the 213 urbanized areas in the United States was nearly 4,000 people per square mile. In the model, A_2 was assigned a value of 0.01 and it produced a population density of about 3,500 people per square mile.

• B_2 (scale parameter in the demand function for housing services): The appropriate value for B_2 depends on the units in which demand for housing services is measured. Given the value of A_2, B_2 should be chosen so that the fraction of income spent on housing services in the model is approximately in accord with the facts. In the United States, the average family spends about 15 percent of its disposable income on housing. In the model, a value for B_2 of 0.10 yielded an expenditure of about this fraction of income on housing services, i.e., if $B_2 = 0.10$, expenditure on housing in the model is about $4.00 per day $[\simeq(.15)(25)]$.

• $L_3(u)$ (function showing the amount of land devoted to transportation at each u): The goal was to choose as realistic a form for $L_3(u)$ as possible, consistent with computational simplicity. In most metropolitan areas the amount of land devoted to transportation increases slightly with distance from the city center, although the fraction of land so used falls rapidly. This pattern was approximated by setting $L_3(u) = L_3$, a constant. L_3 is subject to the restriction $L_3 \leq \phi\epsilon$, since $\phi\epsilon$ represents the total land available at the edge of the CBD. Data presented by Niedercorn and Hearle [28] indicate that about 20 percent of the land in a sample of large United States cities is used for roads and highways. In the model, L_3 was assigned a value of 6.25 because it implies that about 20 percent of the urban area's land is used for transportation. That is, an L_3 of 6.25 implies that 20 percent of the land is used for transportation in a circular city with a 10-mile radius.

• A_3 (scale parameter in the transportation production function): A_3 determines the productivity of the transportation system in the sense that it relates the number of commuters handled by the design capacity of the transportation system to the land devoted to transportation. But there is no absolute limit to the number of commuters that can use a transportation system of any design capacity in the model. What is at stake in the choice of A_3 is the amount of congestion that will be caused by given numbers of commuters. Therefore, A_3 must be chosen in conjunction with the parameters of the congestion function, ρ_1 and ρ_2. In the model, a value of 40,000 was assigned to A_3. Since L_3 is 6.25, it implies that the design capacity of the transportation system is 250,000 $[=(6.25)(40,000)]$. Thus, at the edge of the CBD, where all the 300,000 workers must commute, the ratio of commuting demand to design capacity, which appears in equation (20) of chapter 6, is $1.2(=300,000 \div 250,000)$. The next step is to choose values of the travel-cost parameters so that realistic congestion costs are implied by this ratio.

• $\bar{p}_3$ (two times the cost per mile of commuting in the absence of congestion): A reasonable and common estimate of automobile operating cost for the mid-1960s was $0.10 per vehicle-mile. The time cost of uncongested commuting was estimated as follows. Average weekly earnings were assumed above to be $95, or nearly $2.50 per hour. Assuming an uncongested commuting speed of 25 miles per hour and valuing travel time at the hourly wage rate, two miles of commuting entails a time cost of $0.20 $[=(\$2.50)(1/25)(2)]$. Adding operating and time costs together, we get a value of $0.40 for $\bar{p}_3$. The assumptions imply that uncongested travel cost is equally divided between time and operating costs. There is, of course, great uncertainty about commuters' valuation of travel time. The $0.20 time cost per two miles of travel used here is unaffected by a proportionate change in the assumed values of travel time and travel speed. For example, if travel time were valued at $2.00 per hour and uncongested travel speed were 20 miles per hour, time cost per mile of travel would be unchanged.

• ρ_2 (exponent of congestion cost function): Vickery [33] believes this parameter should have a value of at least two, and a value of two was used in the present study.

• ρ_1 (scale parameter in the congestion cost function): For the purposes of this study, ρ_1 was assigned a value of one. It implies that commuting cost per mile in the most congested part of the urban area, at the edge of the CBD, is almost five times its level in an area free of congestion. It follows from equations (8), (9), and (10) in chapter 6 that cost per two miles of commuting at the edge of the CBD is

$$(1) \qquad p_3(\epsilon) = \bar{p}_3 + \rho_1 \left[\frac{N}{A_3 L_3} \right]^{\rho_2}.$$

Inserting a value of one for ρ_1 and values of the other parameters that were derived above gives a value of $1.84 $[=0.40 + 1(1.20)^2]$ for $p_3(\epsilon)$ in equation (1). It is almost five times as high as the $0.40 cost per two miles of uncongested commuting. The value of ρ_1 seems somewhat high, but precise evaluation is difficult.

For ease of reference, the parameter values chosen above are brought together in table 22.

2. Tabulation of Results

Before presenting the results of the numerical analysis, it is useful to make some remarks about the characteristics of the model that are to be tabulated. The complete solution of the model consists of the values of

Table 22. Parameter Values

Parameter	Value	Parameter	Value
α_2	0.20	ϵ	1
r	0.0005	A_2	0.01
w	25	B_2	0.10
θ_1	1.50	L_3	6.25
θ_2	-1.50	A_3	40,000
R_A	800	$\bar{p}_3$	0.40
N	300,000	ρ_2	2
ϕ	6.28	ρ_1	1

one variable and of eleven functions of u. It would be possible to tabulate each of the eleven functions at one-mile or 0.1-mile intervals. But to do so would be tedious. In addition, some of the functions depend on arbitrary choices of units and therefore convey little intuitive feeling about the urban area the model generates. Others are functions about whose empirical counterparts little is known except for related statistics computed for the urban area as a whole.

The attempt has been made in the sensitivity analysis in section 4 to tabulate a set of characteristics of the urban area generated by the model that would be interesting and informative. The main criterion for informativeness was that the data tabulated be comparable with data available for a large variety of United States urban areas. Following are the eight characteristics selected, the units in which they are measured, and the ways they were computed:

(i) u_A, the radius of the urban area, measured in miles. u_A is computed by the basic iterative procedure described in section 2 of chapter 6.

(ii) The area of the urban area, measured in square miles. The urban area contains $\phi u_A^2 / 2$ square miles.

(iii) Population density, measured in people per square mile of land in the urban area (gross population density). Using a labor force participation rate of one-third, the population of the urban area is $3N = 900,000$. Population density is total population divided by the area of the urban area, i.e., $6N/\phi u_A^2$.

(iv) Percentage of the urban area devoted to the transportation system. A band of width L_3 is devoted to transportation at each u. Therefore the total amount of land devoted to transportation outside the CBD is $L_3(u_A - \epsilon)$. The percentage of the urban area outside the CBD that is devoted to transportation is $2L_3(u_A - \epsilon)/\phi u_A^2$.

(v) $R(\epsilon)$, land rent per square mile of land per working day at the edge of the CBD. $R(\epsilon)$ is computed as described in section 2 of chapter 6. It is the highest point on the rent-distance function computed by the model.

(vi) $R(3)$, land rent per square mile of land per working day three miles from the edge of the CBD. $R(3)$ is also computed by the procedure described in section 2 of chapter 6. There is little point in tabulating a value of $R(u)$ very close to ϵ or to u_A, since those values are known. Furthermore, $R(u)$ is fairly flat near u_A and linear interpolation is a fairly good approximation. But $R(u)$ falls very rapidly near ϵ, and $u = 3$ seemed a good place for a second tabulation of $R(u)$. Along with a knowledge of $R(\epsilon)$, u_A, and R_A, $R(3)$ gives a clear picture of the entire rent-distance function.

(vii) $p_3(\epsilon)/2$, transportation cost per commuter-mile at the edge of the CBD. $p_3(u)$ is the sum of the last two terms in equation (20) of chapter 6. Once the correct value of $R(\epsilon)$ has been found by the procedure described there, the computer prints out $p_3(u)$ for preselected values of u; $p_3(\epsilon)$ shows commuting cost at the most congested part of the city.

(viii) $p_3(3)/2$, transportation cost per commuter-mile three miles from the edge of the CBD. This is computed as described in (vii). It follows from equations (9), (10), and (13) of chapter 6 that $p_3(u_A) = \bar{p}_3$, i.e., congestion disappears at the edge of the urban area. Therefore, along with $p_3(\epsilon)$, $p_3(3)$ gives a fairly complete picture of the entire transportation cost function.

With these results, it is easy to calculate almost all the endogenous functions of the model, using the equations presented in chapter 6. For example, using the values of $R(u)$ tabulated in (v) and (vi) above, $p_2(u)$, the price of housing services can be computed for the same values of u from equation (15) of chapter 6. Likewise, net population density (specifically, workers resident per square mile of land devoted to housing) can be computed for specific values of u from equation (18) of chapter 6. Gross population density can be computed for specific values of u by dividing both sides of equation (18) of chapter 6 by ϕu.

3. Characteristics of the Model

Using the parameter values specified in section 1, the eight characteristics of the model specified in section 2 can be found in table 23.

Table 23 shows that the urban area has a radius of 9.0 miles or a total area of 254 square miles. This implies a gross population density of 3,543 people per square mile. It was stated in section 1 that this is about typical of large urbanized areas in the United States and that values of parameters of the model were chosen to yield this result.

Land rent at the edge of the CBD is \$66,000 per square mile per working day. This is 85 times its level of \$800 at the edge of the urban area. On the assumptions made in section 1, it was shown that a land rent of

Table 23. Characteristics of the Model

(i)	(ii)	(iii)	(iv)	(v)	(vi)	(vii)	(viii)
u_A	Total area	Overall population density	Percent of area devoted to transportation	$R(\epsilon)$	$R(3)$	$\bar{p}_3(\epsilon)/2$	$\bar{p}_3(3)/2$
9.0	254	3,543	19.7	$66,000	$6,040	$0.97	$0.51

$800 per square mile per working day corresponds approximately to a land value of $3,000 per acre. On the same assumptions, a land rent of $66,000 per square mile per day corresponds to a land value of about $255,000 per acre. Land values in downtown areas of large cities often seem to be 50 or 100 times the values at the edge of the urban area. It is interesting and reassuring that the model produces a value that is well within that range. Table 23 shows that three miles from the edge of the CBD, land rent has fallen to $6,040, or to less than eight times its level at the edge of the urban area. Thus, the model also mirrors reality in that land rents fall rapidly near the city center and much less rapidly toward the edge of the urban area.

The last two entries in table 23 show transportation costs per commuter-mile at the edge of the CBD and three miles farther out from the city center. As was stated in section 1, commuting cost at the edge of the CBD is nearly five times its level at the edge of the urban area, where there is no congestion. Since commuting cost per mile is $0.20 in the absence of congestion, it implies that congestion raises travel cost by $0.77 ($0.97 − $0.20) at the edge of the CBD. Three miles farther away, commuting cost has fallen to a little more than half its level at the edge of the CBD. Thus, at $u = 3$, commuting cost is still more than twice as high as its uncongested level of $0.20 per mile.

The land rent and commuting-cost functions are the most interesting in the model. Furthermore, the general form of these functions does not change greatly when the parameters of the model are varied by the amounts considered in the next section. Therefore, in table 24, these functions are tabulated at one-mile intervals for the entire urban area.

Although both land rent and commuting cost fall rapidly with u close to the edge of the CBD, land rent falls much more rapidly than commuting cost. Of the total decrease in land rent from $u = 1$ to $u = 9$, about 75 percent takes place in the first mile from the edge of the CBD. Of the total decrease in commuting cost per mile that takes place from $u = 1$ to $u = 9$, only about one-third takes place in the first mile from the edge of the CBD.

Table 24. Rent Distance and Commuting-Cost Functions

u	$R(u)$	$p_3(u)/2$
1	66,000	0.97
2	14,453	0.71
3	6,640	0.51
4	3,413	0.39
5	2,254	0.32
6	1,631	0.27
7	1,250	0.23
8	992	0.21
9	805	0.20

It is unfortunate that we have little evidence about the way commuting costs vary with distance from the centers of metropolitan areas. It is therefore not possible to know whether the commuting-cost function shown in table 24 is realistic. But we do have at least some evidence that the exponential function explains a large part of the variability of land values with distance from the center in large urban areas (see equation (20) of chapter 6). Indeed, in the present model it follows from equation (18) of chapter 6 that net population density is proportionate to $R(u)$ raised to a constant power. Since an exponential function raised to a power is still an exponential function, it follows that the exponential function will be as good an approximation to the net population density function as it is to the land rent function. (The exponential function will be a similarly good approximation to the gross population density function to the extent that, contrary to the assumption in the present model, the amount of land used for nonresidential purposes is proportionate to u.) Thus it is of considerable interest to see how closely the exponential function approximates the land rent data in table 24. The approximation will be close if the linear regression of log $R(u)$ on u provides a close fit. The regression estimated from the data points in table 24 is

(2) $$\log R(u) = 10.6134 - 0.4925\, u + e .$$
$$(27.57) \quad (-7.20)$$

The squared correlation coefficient between log $R(u)$ and u is 0.8821. Numbers in parentheses are t-statistics. The conclusion is that the exponential function is a good, but not excellent, approximation to the rent-distance function in this model. The actual- lies above the fitted-rent function at very small and very large values of u, indicating that the actual-rent function has more curvature than the fitted-exponential function.

It was shown in chapter 5 that, if housing per capita and transportation cost per passenger mile are constant, and if there is no substitutability between land and other inputs in producing housing, then net population density would be a constant wherever people lived and land rent would be linear in distance from the city center. If the housing production function is Cobb-Douglas, as in the model considered here, and if the price elasticity of per capita demand for housing is minus one, then the land-rent function is exponential in distance from the city center. In the present model, two characteristics combine to produce a land-rent function with more curvature than the exponential. First, housing demand is very elastic and, second, transportation cost per passenger mile falls off with distance from the city center. A conjecture is that, if the housing production function were CES, then an elasticity of substitution between land and capital greater than one would yield even more curvature in the rent function, whereas an elasticity of substitution less than one would yield less curvature than is found in the present model.

4. SENSITIVITY ANALYSIS

The most interesting analysis of the model is to compute the effects of parameter changes on the characteristics of the urban area. The purpose of these computations is to ascertain the directions and magnitudes of the effects of parameter changes on land values, land uses, and congestion. It is appropriate to remind the reader at this point that the comparisons presented in this section are among long-run equilibrium positions and that, as the evidence presented in chapter 3 indicated, adjustment times are likely to be long.

It was decided to change each parameter by ±20 percent and to recompute for each set of parameter values each of the eight characteristics of the urban area presented in section 3. There is no guarantee that either the amounts or the percentages of changes in the dependent variables would vary proportionately if the effects of other parameter changes were computed. It is even possible that some of the signs would be different.

The results of the sensitivity analysis are in table 25. Columns in table 25 have the same meanings as they have in table 23. Roman numerals beside rows indicate the parameter that has been changed. In each row, all other parameters have the values assigned to them in section 1. Row I of table 25 repeats the information about the original model from table 23, for ease of reference. Numbers in parentheses indicate the percentage by which each parameter or characteristic differs from its value in the initial model. For example, the entry at the top of row V and column (iii) indicates that a 20 percent decrease in B_2 has caused a 33 percent increase in overall population density. Thus, the elasticity of overall population density with respect to B_2 is 1.65. There is, of course, no presumption that any such elasticities calculated from table 25 are independent of the set of parameter values chosen.

There are two exceptions to the rule that each parameter was varied by ± 20 percent. First, many characteristics of the model proved to be extremely sensitive to changes in θ_1. In order to be able to find the new solution of the model within a reasonable time, it was decided to vary θ_1 by only ± 10 percent. Second, L_3 cannot be increased because it would violate the inequality $L_3 \leq \phi\epsilon$, which is a physical constraint on the system.

Before detailed comments are made on the results in table 25, a few general remarks should be made. First, total urban area is inevitably more sensitive to parameter changes than is the radius of the urban area, since the former is proportionate to the square of the latter. Second, $R(\epsilon)$ is generally the most sensitive of the characteristics in table 25, although the reason is not clear. It is, however, plausible that $R(\epsilon)$ should be more sensitive than $R(3)$. $R(u)$ falls eventually to R_A and is therefore less sensitive to most parameter changes at large values of u than at small values. Third, in most rows in table 25, population density and $R(\epsilon)$ move in the same direction, and this direction is opposite from that in which the radius and total area of the urban area move. Whatever causes land rent to rise also causes a decrease in total housing demand and in land input per unit output of housing services. Both effects cause a decrease in the size of the urban area, and a consequent increase in population density. An exception to this generalization occurs when the cause of the changes is a change in N. For a fixed N, an increase in overall population density must imply a steepening of the population density function. As long as R_A is unchanged, population density at u_A is unchanged. Therefore an increase in overall density must mean that the increase is concentrated near the city center. Fourth, although there are several exceptions, there is a tendency for $R(\epsilon)$ and $R(3)$ to move in opposite directions. This is an implication of the fact that $R(\epsilon)$ and u_A tend to move in opposite directions. If $R(\epsilon)$ increases, but falls to R_A at a smaller value of u than previously, then $R(u)$ must be below its previous value for large values of u. Fifth, it follows from equation (1) in this chapter that $p_3(\epsilon)$ is affected only by $\bar{p}_3$, ρ_1, ρ_2, N, A_3 and L_3. Therefore column (vii) remains unchanged in response to changes in other parameters, while $p_3(3)$ is affected by all parameters. Sixth, the percentage of the urban area devoted to transportation generally moves in the opposite direction from the size of the urban area. Land devoted to transportation is proportionate to u_A, whereas area of the urban area is proportionate to the square of u_A. Therefore, the ratio moves in the opposite direction from the denominator. Seventh,

Table 25. Sensitivity Analysis

Parameter set	(i) u_A	(ii) Total area	(iii) Overall population density	(iv) Percent of area devoted to transportation	(v) $R(\epsilon)$	(vi) $R(3)$	(vii) $p_3(\epsilon)/2$	(viii) $p_3(3)/2$
I Initial	9.0	254	3,543	19.7	66,000	6,040	0.97	0.51
II								
$A_2 = 0.008$ (−20)	8.4 (−7)	222 (−13)	4,054 (+14)	20.7 (+5)	78,500 (+19)	5,638 (−7)	0.97 (0)	0.47 (−8)
$A_2 = 0.012$ (+20)	9.6 (+7)	289 (+14)	3,114 (−12)	18.7 (−5)	58,000 (−12)	6,394 (+6)	0.97 (0)	0.54 (+6)
III								
$\alpha_2 = 0.16$ (−20)	9.6 (+7)	289 (+14)	3,114 (−12)	18.7 (−5)	52,300 (−21)	6,581 (+9)	0.97 (0)	0.57 (+12)
$\alpha_2 = 0.24$ (+20)	8.1 (−10)	206 (−19)	4,370 (+23)	21.4 (+9)	91,500 (+39)	5,243 (−13)	0.97 (0)	0.45 (−12)
IV								
$A_3 = 32,000$ (−20)	8.8 (−2)	243 (−4)	3,704 (+5)	20.2 (+3)	170,000 (+158)	5,769 (−4)	1.36 (+40)	0.55 (+8)
$A_3 = 48,000$ (+20)	9.3 (+3)	272 (+7)	3,309 (−7)	19.1 (−3)	37,200 (−44)	5,989 (−1)	0.74 (−24)	0.46 (−10)
V								
$B_2 = 0.08$ (−20)	7.8 (−13)	191 (−25)	4,712 (+33)	22.5 (+14)	94,000 (+42)	5,164 (−15)	0.97 (0)	0.44 (−14)
$B_2 = 0.12$ (+20)	10.1 (+12)	320 (+26)	2,813 (−21)	17.8 (−10)	51,000 (−23)	6,680 (+11)	0.97 (0)	0.58 (+14)

	(1)	(2)	(3)	(4)	(5)	(6)	(7)	(8)
VI								
$\theta_1 = 1.35$ (−10)	6.5 (−28)	133 (−48)	6,767 (+91)	25.9 (+31)	155,000 (+135)	4,110 (−32)	0.97 (0)	0.36 (−29)
$\theta_1 = 1.65$ (+10)	12.4 (+38)	483 (+90)	1,863 (−47)	14.8 (−25)	35,100 (−47)	7,557 (+25)	0.97 (0)	0.68 (+33)
VII								
$\theta_2 = 12$ (−20)	10.1 (+12)	320 (+26)	2,813 (−21)	17.8 (−10)	43,800 (−34)	7,159 (+19)	0.97 (0)	0.60 (+18)
$\theta_2 = -1.8$ (+20)	8.2 (−9)	211 (−17)	4,265 (+20)	21.3 (+8)	125,000 (+89)	4,934 (−18)	0.97 (0)	0.42 (−18)
VIII								
$r = 0.0004$ (−20)	9.5 (+6)	283 (+11)	3,180 (−10)	18.7 (−5)	58,000 (−12)	6,363 (+5)	0.97 (0)	0.64 (+25)
$r = 0.0006$ (+20)	8.7 (−3)	238 (−6)	3,782 (+7)	20.2 (+3)	74,000 (+12)	5,801 (−4)	0.97 (0)	0.48 (−6)
IX								
$w = 20$ (−20)	7.2 (−20)	163 (−36)	5,521 (+56)	23.9 (+21)	115,000 (+74)	4,728 (−22)	0.97 (0)	0.40 (−22)
$w = 30$ (+20)	11.1 (+23)	387 (+52)	2,326 (−34)	16.3 (−17)	46,000 (−30)	7,113 (+18)	0.97 (0)	0.60 (+18)
X								
$R_A = 640$ (−20)	10.0 (+11)	314 (+24)	2,866 (−19)	17.8 (−10)	65,500 (−1)	5,972 (−1)	0.97 (0)	0.52 (+2)
$R_A = 960$ (+20)	8.6 (−4)	232 (−9)	3,879 (+9)	20.7 (+5)	67,500 (+2)	6,246 (+3)	0.97 (0)	0.50 (−2)
XI								
$\bar{p}_3 = 0.32$ (−20)	9.9 (+10)	308 (+21)	2,922 (−18)	18.2 (−8)	57,200 (−13)	5,858 (−3)	0.93 (−4)	0.50 (−2)
$\bar{p}_3 = 0.48$ (+20)	8.6 (−4)	232 (−9)	3,879 (+9)	20.7 (+5)	77,000 (+17)	6,334 (+5)	1.01 (+4)	0.52 (+2)

121

Table 25. Continued

Parameter set	(i) u_A	(ii) Total area	(iii) Overall population density	(iv) Percent of area devoted to transportation	(v) $R(\epsilon)$	(vi) $R(3)$	(vii) $p_3(\epsilon)/2$	(viii) $p_3(3)/2$
XII								
$\rho_1 = 0.8$ (−20)	9.3 (+3)	272 (+7)	3,309 (−7)	19.1 (−3)	46,000 (−30)	6,088 (+1)	0.82 (−15)	0.48 (−6)
$\rho_1 = 1.2$ (+20)	9.0 (0)	254 (0)	3,543 (0)	19.7 (0)	94,000 (+42)	6,045 (0)	1.11 (+14)	0.51 (0)
XIII								
$\rho_2 = 1.6$ (−20)	8.9 (−1)	249 (−2)	3,614 (+2)	19.7 (0)	65,500 (−1)	6,533 (+8)	0.90 (−7)	0.52 (+2)
$\rho_2 = 2.4$ (+20)	9.2 (+2)	266 (+5)	3,383 (−5)	19.2 (−3)	69,000 (+5)	5,753 (−5)	1.04 (+7)	0.50 (−2)
XIV								
$L_3 = 5.0$ (−20)	8.8 (−2)	243 (−4)	3,704 (+5)	16.0 (−19)	96,500 (+46)	5,360 (−11)	1.25 (+29)	0.52 (+2)
XV								
$N = 240,000$ (−20)	8.9 (−1)	249 (−2)	2,892 (−18)	19.8 (+1)	27,500 (−58)	5,129 (−15)	0.70 (−28)	0.44 (−14)
$N = 360,000$ (+20)	9.1 (+1)	260 (+2)	4,337 (+22)	19.5 (−1)	170,500 (+158)	6,695 (+11)	1.28 (+32)	0.55 (+8)

several of the parameter changes indicate substantial changes in the form of the land-rent and population-density functions. These results suggest strongly that special functional forms used for such relationships, such as the exponential form used in chapter 3 and by many other writers, are at best approximate and descriptive.

Specific comments follow on each of the parameter changes shown in table 25.

Row II. An increase in A_2 represents neutral disembodied technical progress in the production of housing services. It means that the previous output of housing services can now be produced with smaller inputs of capital and land. Surprisingly, the effect of an increase in A_2 is to increase the size of the urban area. There seem to be two explanations. First, $R(\epsilon)$ falls, which means cheaper and more land-intensive housing services, and the high price elasticity of demand for housing services means a large increase in the demand for land for housing. Second, the lower price of housing changes the trade-off between housing and commuting in the direction of more housing and therefore more commuting. The result, as indicated by column (viii), is a slight increase in congestion costs at $u = 3$. Although it is not usually mentioned in the literature, the results discussed in this paragraph suggest that technical progress in the production of housing services may be a cause of decentralization in urban areas.

Row III. An increase in α_2 means an increase in the productivity and share of land, and a corresponding decrease for capital, in the production of housing services. Economic intuition does not provide a clear indication of the likely effects on the urban area of a change in α_2. But it is interesting to observe that an increase in α_2 decreases the size of the urban area substantially and increases $R(\epsilon)$ by a large amount. The result is a decrease in $p_3(3)$. Intuitive understanding of the effects of changing α_2 is confounded by the fact that, within the constraint of constant returns, an increase in land's productivity is also a decrease in capital's productivity. But the results in row III are generally those that would be expected from an exogenous change in land rent, e.g., a change in R_A. When α_2 goes up, the urban area economizes on the use of land to produce housing and concentrates the housing closer to the city center.

Row IV. An increase in A_3 represents technical progress in the supply of transportation. Predictably, the resulting increase in the capacity of the transportation system induces workers to use more transportation by moving farther out, and it drastically reduces $R(\epsilon)$. Congestion cost falls at both $u = \epsilon$ and $u = 3$. In this model, an improvement in the transportation system causes the urban area to decentralize and land rents to fall near the city center. These results accord with the anticipations of Clark [5] and suggest that city center landowners may suffer as a result of improved urban transportation.

Row V. An increase in B_2 means an increase in per capita demand for housing services at given levels of housing price and income. Not surprisingly, an increase in B_2 increases the size of the urban area and reduces density. These changes inevitably increase congestion costs at $u = 3$. It is, however, surprising and inexplicable that an increase in B_2 should reduce $R(\epsilon)$.

Row VI. An increase in θ_1 increases the income elasticity of demand for housing services, but it also increases the amount of housing services demanded at given price and income levels. Not surprisingly, an increase in θ_1 increases the size of the urban area and reduces population density. The sensitivity is, however, surprising. A 10 percent increase in θ_1 results in a 90 percent increase in total area. Likewise, it is surprising that an increase in θ_1 leads to a decrease in $R(\epsilon)$. It undoubtedly has to do with the behavior of equation (7) of chapter 6, representing the trade-off between housing and commuting costs.

Row VII. An increase in the absolute value of θ_2 represents an increase in the own price elasticity of demand for housing services; it also represents a change in the amount of housing services demanded at each price. At prices greater than one, the demand for housing services decreases as θ_2 increases in absolute value; at prices less than one the demand increases as θ_2 increases in absolute value. The parameter values used here imply that $p_2(u)$ exceeds one at each u. Therefore an increase in the absolute value of θ_2 from 1.5 to 1.8 means a decrease in housing service demand, and the results are parallel to those observed in V and VI when parameters changed so as to reduce housing demand.

Row VIII. An increase in r means an increase in the rental rate on capital. Not surprisingly, it reduces the size of the urban area, increases its density, and increases $R(\epsilon)$. The last results from the attempt to substitute land for capital in producing housing services, which drives up land rents. Congestion cost is decreased at $u = 3$ because housing has become more concentrated near the city center, and therefore fewer people live beyond $u = 3$.

Row IX. An increase in w represents an increase in income, which increases the demand for housing, enlarges the urban area, and reduces density. Again, it is surprising that $R(\epsilon)$ falls, but not that $R(3)$ rises. It should be noted that the opportunity cost of time spent traveling, which is included in $\bar{p}_3$, has not been changed as w was changed in IX. But a comparison between IX and XI shows that the model is much more sensitive to changes in w than to changes in $\bar{p}_3$, presumably because of the high income elasticity of demand for housing. Thus, an increase in w combined with an increase in $\bar{p}_3$ would undoubtedly have a net effect of causing the urban area to decentralize and population density to fall. This reasoning suggests that increases in income have probably been a major reason for the flattening of population density functions recorded in chapter 3.

Row X. An increase in R_A represents an increase in the opportunity cost of using land for urban purposes. It is therefore plausible that the results should be a decrease in the size of the urban area, an increase in its density, and an increase in urban land rents. The surprising characteristic of these calculations is the insensitivity of the model to changes in R_A.

Row XI. An increase in $\bar{p}_3$ represents an increase in the cost of un-congested travel. It should be expected that the increase will lead to an increase in the population density and to a decrease in the size of the urban area. It is interesting that travel cost per commuter-mile at $u = 3$ is so insensitive to $\bar{p}_3$. The increase in $\bar{p}_3$ causes adjustments in the urban area that reduce congestion at $u = 3$, and $p_3(3)$ therefore changes relatively little. Likewise, $p_3(\epsilon)$ is also insensitive to $\bar{p}_3$. Travel cost is predominantly congestion cost in the present model and changes in the cost of uncongested travel therefore have relatively little effect on urban structure.

Row XII. An increase in ρ_1 means an increase in travel cost resulting from given amounts of congestion. Most characteristics of the model are extremely insensitive to changes in ρ_1. For unknown reasons, decreases in ρ_1 produced small increases in the size of the urban area, but increases in ρ_1 produced no change in size. Both increases and decreases did, however, produce large changes in $R(\epsilon)$, although practically no change in $R(3)$. The effects of ρ_1 on $p_3(\epsilon)$ can be verified from (1) of section 1.

Row XIII. An increase in ρ_2 means an increase in the elasticity of congestion cost with respect to the amount of congestion. If

$$X_{3D}(u)/X_{3S}(u) > 1,$$

an increase in ρ_2 also increases the level of congestion costs resulting from a given amount of congestion. But, if

$$X_{3D}(u)/X_{3S}(u) < 1,$$

then increasing ρ_2 reduces congestion cost at given levels of congestion. These properties of the congestion cost function account for the paradoxi-cal appearance of the results in row XIII. An increase in ρ_2 increases congestion cost at $u = \epsilon$, where

$$X_{3D}(u)/X_{3S}(u) > 1,$$

but it decreases congestion cost at $u = 3$, where the opposite inequality holds. Thus, travel cost falls far from the city center and the result is a small movement to decentralize and enlarge the urban area.

Row XIV. A decrease in L_3 means a decrease in the land devoted to transportation at each u. The result is to make the transportation system more congested and to raise transportation costs at both $u = \epsilon$ and $u = 3$. It leads the urban area to economize on transportation by increasing the population density and shrinking the size of the urban area. It also leads to the expected increase in $R(\epsilon)$.

Row XV. An increase in N means an exogenous increase in the urban area's population. Not surprisingly, it leads to an increase in the size and population density of the urban area. It also leads to an increase in both $R(u)$ and $p_3(u)$ at both $u = \epsilon$ and $u = 3$. It is interesting to note that $R(\epsilon)$ is extremely sensitive to N. Although employment suburbanization is not included in the present model, it suggests that extremely high central land values provide strong incentives for employers to suburbanize when the urban area reaches a modest population.

5. Comparison with Earlier Model

This chapter will conclude with a brief comparison between the results in the preceding section and a similar sensitivity analysis of an earlier model. The earlier model is presented and analyzed in Mills [19]. The sensitivity analysis is reported in Mills and Dee [23].

The present model differs from the earlier one in three major respects. First, inputs and outputs in CBD production were endogenous in the earlier model, whereas they are exogenous in the present model. This means, in particular, that the urban area's labor force was endogenous in the earlier model. Second, the transportation system was much less developed and realistic in the earlier model than in the present one. Land allocation to transportation was endogenous in the earlier model and it was assumed that enough land was allocated to transportation to meet whatever demands were made upon it. Transportation cost was proportionate to the rent of land used for transportation. Thus, there was no congestion and no time cost of transportation. Third, there was no demand side in the market for housing services in the earlier model. Instead, it was assumed that the consumption of housing services per worker was an exogenous constant.

In view of the extensive differences between the two models, there is little reason to expect the results of the sensitivity analysis to be similar, and a detailed comparison will not be presented here. But several paradoxical properties appeared in the earlier model, and it is worthwhile to ascertain whether they resulted from peculiarities in that model.

The most paradoxical property of the earlier model was that exogenous increases in the wage rate and the rental rate on capital had the effect of increasing the urban area's population, output, and land area. Economic intuition suggests that exogenous increases in factor prices should cause output, factor use, and the size of the urban area to shrink. These paradoxical results are absent from the present model. The effects of the wage rate are quite different in the two models. In the earlier model, the effect of a change in the wage rate was entirely on the supply side in that the demand for labor was affected. In the present model, the wage rate (or income) appears only as a variable in the demand function for housing services. The rental rate of capital appears in a similar way in the two models, and it is unclear why the effects of its change are in opposite directions.

A second important difference between the two models has to do with the effects of technical change on the production of housing services. In the earlier model, an increase in the efficiency parameter in the production function for housing services reduced the size of the urban area, whereas in the present model the effect of the same change is to increase the size of the urban area. But the result in the earlier model is to be expected in a model in which a reduction in housing prices leads to no increase in housing demand per family. In the present model, the opposite effect of technical change in housing is presumably the result of the elastic demand that was assumed for housing services.

The final difference between the two models that justifies comment has to do with the effect of technical change in the production of transportation. A characteristic shared by the two models is that they are both insensitive to this parameter. But in the earlier model, technical progress in transportation slightly reduced the size of the urban area, whereas in the present model the effect is a slight increase. The property of the earlier model is the implausible one, and it disappears in the present model.

A fair summary would seem to be that although some of the properties of the present model are counterintuitive they are much more in accord with economic intuition than were properties of the earlier model.

8

A Model with an Efficient
Transportation System

The model studied in chapters 6 and 7 was intended to contain several aspects of a realistic transportation system. The design capacity of the transportation system was exogenous to the model, but the use made of it was determined by the individual self-interest of commuters. Commuting was entirely determined by residential location, which in turn depended on housing and commuting costs. In equilibrium, commuting produced an amount of congestion such that travel and housing costs satisfied a certain locational equilibrium condition—equation (7) of chapter 6. It was shown in chapter 7 that considerable congestion and high commuting costs near the city center resulted from the model. It was pointed out in chapter 6 that such a transportation system is inefficient in the Paretian welfare sense in that social cost exceeds private cost at the margin.

The evaluation and improvement of the efficiency of urban transportation systems are certainly among the most pressing problems of our time. The issues are extraordinarily complex. Most urban transportation studies take as given the set of trip origins and destinations and attempt to evaluate benefits and costs of alternative modes. Many studies end with conjectures about the effects of the urban transportation system on the locations of residences and employment. But there has been hardly any systematic evaluation of the effects of urban transportation costs on location decisions. The purpose of this chapter is to study one part of this complex issue within the framework of the model developed in chapter 6. Here, it is asked what the effect on the structure of the urban area would be if resources were allocated to transportation and the facilities were priced in a way that satisfied the usual efficiency conditions of welfare economics. Specifically, suppose that each commuter were permitted to use the transportation system only if he paid the rental cost of his share of transportation land, and suppose that as much land were allocated to the transportation system as could be paid for in this way. How different would the urban area be from the one portrayed in the previous chapter?

It is important to be clear as to what will and will not be demonstrated in this chapter.

Much of the controversy about urban transportation has to do either with the relationships between inputs and outputs for various modes of transportation, i.e., with production functions, or with the characteristics of demand for various modes of transportation. What combination of fares and service will persuade what percentage of commuters to use what form of public transportation? The analysis in this chapter sheds light on neither of these issues. The production and demand functions are the ones represented by equations (8) and (9) of chapter 6, and no new evidence is presented as to their properties. Instead, the technology of the transportation system is taken as given and the effect of an efficient transportation pricing scheme on residential location is studied.

The assumptions about supply and pricing of transportation facilities that are made in the next section obey all the usual conditions of competitive markets. Likewise, the assumptions about the housing market that were made in chapter 6 and are retained here also obey the usual competitive conditions. These facts suggest strongly that the resulting pattern of residential location and commuting must be efficient in the welfare sense. And the arguments analogous to those used in chapter 5 suggest strongly that no changes in location could make any resident better off without making another resident worse off. Nevertheless, the modifications introduced here do not permit any congestion regardless of conditions, which is not optimum in a realistic model. A general analysis of optimality in an urban transportation system has yet to appear.

Finally, even if the optimality of the model in this chapter were established, it might be that optimality resulted only because the model ignored a certain real world cost, namely the cost of metering and therefore charging for the use of particular segments of the urban transportation system. The model in this chapter assumes that use of each segment of the transportation system is priced to reflect opportunity cost. This is not done in practice partly because it is expensive to meter the use of particular road segments. But that expense is ignored in the model. Thus, the analysis in this chapter must be interpreted as an attempt to answer the question: What would be the effect on urban structure if it were possible costlessly to charge opportunity cost for the use of the urban transportation system?

1. MODIFICATION OF THE MODEL

The only modifications to be made here in the model presented in chapter 6 have to do with the supply and pricing of transportation facilities. Equations (1)–(7) of chapter 6 pertaining to the nontransportation parts of the model, are assumed to continue to hold. In addition, the production and demand functions for transportation, equations (8) and (9) of chapter 6 continue to hold. Equations (11) and (13) are also retained.

The modification of the model consists in assuming that the production and pricing decisions concerning transportation services are made as though transportation services were a competitive industry. Specifically, the price of transportation services at each u is the marginal (equals average) cost of the scarce land resources used, and enough facilities are provided to equate supply of and demand for transportation services. Thus, equation (10) of chapter 6 is dropped, and it is replaced by

(1) $$p_3(u) = A_3^{-1}R(u),$$

and

(2) $$X_{3D}(u) = X_{3S}(u).$$

Here and in what follows all symbols have the same meanings assigned to them in chapter 6. One equation has been dropped and two have been added. But, another function from the model, $L_3(u)$, has been added to the list of endogenous functions in the system. The unknowns in the system now consist of u_A, the eleven functions of u listed in section 1 of chapter 6, and $L_3(u)$. Equations (1), (9), and (11) of chapter 6, and (2) of this chapter are twelve simultaneous equations relating the twelve functions of u, and equations (12) and (13) of chapter 6 provide a solution for u_A and an initial condition for $R(u)$.

Using equation (8) of chapter 6, the total cost of the transportation services produced at u is

$$R(u)L_3(u) = A_3^{-1}R(u)X_{3S}(u).$$

Marginal cost is therefore $A_3^{-1}R(u)$. Thus, marginal cost and average cost are equal to each other and to $p_3(u)$ at each u.

2. Solution of the Modified Model

Despite the fact that the modified model has one more equation and one more endogenous function than the complex model, it is much simpler to analyze. Most of the complexity of the earlier model arose from the representation of congestion, and that has now been replaced by a well-behaved competitive industry.

In fact, in this model it is easy to obtain an explicit solution of the land rent function $R(u)$. The substitutions that lead to equation (20) of chapter 6 now lead to

(3) $$\bar{D}R(u)^{\alpha-1}R'(u) + 1 = 0,$$

where

$$\bar{D} = A_3 D$$

and α and D have the meanings assigned to them in chapter 6. Using the initial condition $R(u_A) = R_A$, (3) has the solution

(4) $$R(u) = [R_A^\alpha + \alpha\bar{D}^{-1}(u_A - u)^{\frac{1}{\alpha}}, \qquad\qquad \alpha \neq -1$$

(5) $$R(u) = R_A e^{\bar{D}^{-1}(u_A-u)}. \qquad\qquad \alpha = -1$$

Thus, in this model $R(u)$ is exponential in precisely the case considered by Muth,[1] namely a price elasticity of demand for housing services of minus one. (If $\alpha_2 > 0$, $\theta_2 = -1$ is necessary and sufficient for $\alpha = -1$, since $\alpha = \alpha_2(1 + \theta_2) - 1$.) In this model, it is easy to show that the capital-land ratio in producing housing services and net population density are also exponential if $R(u)$ is. Equation (5) permits an exact determination of the effects of parameters in the system on the intercept and gradient of the exponential rent function. Most of the model's parameters affect $\bar{D}$ and therefore the gradient of equation (5). In addition, u_A is endogenous to the model. All the parameters of the system affect it and, therefore, the intercept of equation (5). Actually, the case in which the price elasticity of demand for housing services is exactly minus one can hardly be of great intrinsic interest. In other cases, equation (4) is an exact solution and approximates (5) when θ_2 is close to minus one. Thus, the main interest of (5) is as an approximation in applied work, where its importance is great. It will not be considered further in this chapter.

In this model, as in the more complex one studied in the last two chapters, all the endogenous functions can be found easily once the land-rent function is fully specified. Thus, the major remaining task is to find a formula to compute u_A in equation (4). The rest of this section is devoted to that task.

Substituting equations (8) and (9) of chapter 6 in equation (2), we get

(6) $$\int_\epsilon^u N(u')du' + A_3 L_3(u) = N.$$

Now, equation (8) of chapter 6 holds for the present model. Using it and equation (11) of chapter 6, we can write equation (6) as

(7) $$\int_\epsilon^u N(u')du' + A_3[\phi u - GN(u)R(u)^\alpha] = N.$$

---

1. See [26] and the discussion in chapter 4.

Putting $u = u_A$ in equation (7), and using equations (12) and (13) of chapter 6, gives

(8) $$N(u_A) = \phi G^{-1} R_A^{-\alpha} u_A,$$

which provides an initial condition for the unknown function $N(u)$.

We can find $N(u)$ explicitly as follows. Differentiating equation (7) with respect to u, we get

(9) $$N(u) + A_3\phi - A_3 G[N(u)\alpha R(u)^{\alpha-1} R'(u) + N'(u) R(u)^\alpha] = 0.$$

Using equations (3) and (4), we can write (9) as

(10) $$(1 + A_3 G \bar{D}^{-1}\alpha) N(u) - A_3 G[R_A^\alpha + \alpha \bar{D}^{-1}(u_A - u)] N'(u) + A_3\phi = 0.$$

Equation (10) is now a differential equation involving only one unknown function, $N(u)$. After rearranging terms, and using the initial condition (8), its solution can be written

(11) $$N(u) = \phi\left[\frac{u_A}{GR_A^\alpha} + \frac{A_3}{1+\alpha}\right]\left[\frac{R_A^\alpha + \alpha \bar{D}^{-1}(u_A - u)}{R_A^\alpha}\right]^{\frac{-1+\alpha}{\alpha}} - \frac{A_3\phi}{1+\alpha}$$
$$= \left[N(u_A) + \frac{\phi A_3}{1+\alpha}\right]\left[\frac{R(u)}{R_A^\alpha}\right]^{-(1+\alpha)} - \frac{A_3\phi}{1+\alpha}.$$

The last equation makes use of (4) and (8). If we put $u = u_A$ in (11), again use (8), and again rearrange terms, we get

(12) $$(1 + \alpha) N + \phi A_3(u_A - \epsilon) - \phi R_A^\alpha A_3[(1 + \alpha) R_A^{-\alpha} u_A + A_3 G]$$
$$\left[1 - \left(\frac{R_A^\alpha + \alpha G^{-1} A_3^{-1}(u_A - \epsilon)}{R_A}\right)^{-\frac{1}{\alpha}}\right] = 0.$$

Equation (12) contains only parameters of the model and the single unknown variable u_A. Thus, finding u_A in this model requires only computation of roots of (12) and does not involve an iterative procedure to compute the entire function $R(u)$ such as was used to find u_A in the complex model in chapter 7. A simple computer program was used to find u_A in the calculations reported in the next section. Problems did not arise with multiple roots, since (12) had only one root in the range of values of u_A considered, roughly $0 \leq u_A \leq 20$. Once u_A has been computed from (12), $R(u)$ can be computed from (4).

Before this section is concluded, a comment should be made concerning the population density function in this model. Equation (18) of chapter 6 shows that net population density is proportionate to a power of $R(u)$. Using equation (4), we see that

(13) $$\frac{L_2(u)}{N(u)} = G[R_A^\alpha + \alpha \bar{D}^{-1}(u_A - u)].$$

Equation (13) shows that the reciprocal of net population density, i.e., residential land per capita, is linear in distance from the city center; it provides a particularly convenient form for empirical estimation and testing. Equation (4) implies that $R(u)$ is a decreasing function of u, while equation (18) of chapter 6 implies that net population density also decreases as u increases ($\alpha < 0$ is implied by $0 \leq \alpha_2 \leq 1$ and $\theta_2 < 0$).

3. Comparison with the Complex Model

In this section a brief comparison is presented between the properties of the complex model studied in chapters 6 and 7 and the modified model presented in this chapter. The purpose is to discover how the introduction of efficient pricing and resource allocation in transportation affects the structure of the urban area. Before the comparison is presented, two points must be made.

First, $\bar{p}_3$, the cost per two miles of uncongested travel in the complex model, plays no role in the modified model. In the complex model, it included a charge for the use of the transportation facilities by commuters, and that charge is represented by (1) in the modified model. Also, inclusion of $\bar{p}_3$ in (1) makes the modified model much more complicated. In the comparison below, $\bar{p}_3$ is set equal to zero in the complex model. The implication is that, in the calculations presented below, congestion cost is the only travel cost included in the complex model. Travel cost in the modified model is of course given by (1). All the other parameters in the model have the values assigned to them in section 1 of chapter 7. Using the data presented in table 25 on the sensitivity of the model to changes in $\bar{p}_3$, it is possible to get a fairly accurate approximation to the solution of the model for values of $\bar{p}_3$ between zero and the value used in chapter 7 ($0.40) by interpolating between table 25 and table 26.

Second, the effect on the model of making the supply side of the transportation system endogenous depends on the amount of land that was allocated to it when it was exogenous. Allocating less land to transportation in the modified model than in the complex model will, other things equal, make the urban area smaller. Allocating more land to transportation in the modified than in the complex model will make the urban

Table 26. Properties of the Complex and Modified Models

Model	(i) u_A	(ii) Total area	(iii) Overall population density	(iv) Percent of area devoted to transportation	(v) $R(\epsilon)$	(vi) $R(3)$	(vii) $p_3(\epsilon)/2$	(viii) $p_3(3)/2$
Complex	12.5	491	1,833	14.6	$28,200	$4,365	$0.77	$0.48
Modified	16.1	814	1,106	8.6	937	916	0.09	0.02

area larger. Although the land allocated to transportation in the complex model was chosen to be representative of large U.S. urban areas, the choice was arbitrary in the sense that there is no criterion in that model for an optimum allocation of land to transportation.

Putting $\bar{p}_3 = 0$ in the complex model, but otherwise using the parameter values chosen in chapter 7 for both models, the characteristics of the urban areas produced by the two models are presented in table 26. The characteristics presented and the units in which they are tabulated are as described in chapter 7. The calculations for the complex model were performed as described in chapters 6 and 7. For the modified model, u_A was computed from equation (12), land used for transportation was approximated using (6) and (11), $R(\epsilon)$ and $R(3)$ were computed from (4), $p_3(\epsilon)$ and $p_3(3)$ were computed from (1), and the other characteristics were computed as described in chapter 7.

The data in table 26 for the complex model show that putting $\bar{p}_3$ equal to zero has a considerable effect on the urban area. Comparison with table 23 indicates that the urban area is now larger and has lower density, land rents, and transportation costs. The qualitative changes are those that should be expected from an exogenous reduction in transportation costs.

The clear message in table 26 is that the modified model produces a much larger and lower density urban area than the complex model. The modified model has almost two-thirds more area than the complex model and almost one-third lower population density. $R(\epsilon)$ is much smaller in the modified than in the complex model and transportation costs are correspondingly lower.

Although the total amount of land used for transportation is about the same in the two models (about 70 square miles), it is a much smaller percentage of the land in the larger urban area produced by the modified model. One reason is that in the complex model some of the land devoted to transportation is in the wrong place, i.e., near the edge of the urban area, whereas in the modified model land is devoted to transportation only where it is needed. But a second reason is that inefficient pricing of transportation services in the complex model results in very high congestion costs. Despite the fact that transportation cost goes to zero at u_A in the complex model, overall transportation costs are much higher in that model than in the modified model. It is interesting to note that the amount of land devoted to transportation at the edge of the CBD is practically the same in the two models. The parameter values used in chapter 7 were such that $X_{3D}(\epsilon) = N$ differed little from $X_{3S}(\epsilon) = \alpha_3 L_3$.

Within the context of the assumptions made in the two models being compared, the inevitable conclusion is that improper pricing of urban transportation services leads to large distortions in the allocation of resources. Congestion makes transportation expensive, with the result that residents are induced to avoid long commuting trips by living close to downtown places of work. The attempt to concentrate housing close to the CBD, in turn, bids up land values there.

No one should regard as realistic the magnitude of the distortion from improper pricing of transportation services that has been found here. Putting $\bar{p}_3$ equal to zero means that transportation cost depends only on land rent in the modified model. It makes transportation costs and hence residential density extremely sensitive to land rent. A more realistic model would presumably indicate less sensitivity. Furthermore, the different characteristics of the urban areas in the complex and modified models result to an unknown extent from the different representation of transportation costs in the two models.

4. Concluding Remarks

Some readers may be surprised at the conclusion that efficient pricing of transportation services and the consequent reduction in transportation costs result in more rather than less decentralization of the metropolitan area. The purpose of this section is to speculate on the reasonableness of the conclusion outside the framework of the models studied in this book.

The purpose of improved pricing in an urban transportation system is to increase the system's efficiency. For the purpose of this discussion, suppose that a change is introduced that reduces the cost of radial travel, whether the change be improved pricing, a public transit system, or a radial expressway. The change will affect three groups of workers.

First, those who formerly worked in or near the CBD will find that their real incomes have risen and that the cost of commuting has fallen in relation to prices of other goods and services, including leisure. This group's behavior has been analyzed in this and the preceding chapters. It seems indisputable that the change will induce them to commute longer distances, which they will accomplish by flattening the urban area's residential density function.

Second, as was documented in chapter 3, many urban residents work outside the CBD, although it was excluded from the models analyzed here. CBD locations will be made more attractive to suburban employers by the transportation improvement, since the CBD has become more accessible. Presumably, some formerly suburban employment will move downtown. Such workers will find themselves living farther from their places of work than before and will, on the average, move closer to the CBD. The effect will be to increase the steepness of the residential density function. Those who expect transportation improvements to increase urban densities appear to rely mainly on the size of this effect. Although one cannot be sure, there is reason to doubt whether the effect of improved urban transportation on movement of employment from suburb to CBDs is likely to be substantial. The data presented in chapter 3 and other evidence suggest that the major causes of employment suburbanization have been the rapid increase in intercity freight movement by road, which removes the need for location near downtown transportation terminals, and population suburbanization caused by rising incomes. If these variables are indeed the main causes of employment suburbanization, urban transportation improvements will hardly affect the trend. Only if poor access to the CBD has been a major cause of employment suburbanization will transportation improvements affect the trend.

Third, improved radial transportation might attract more employment to the metropolitan area. Improvements in an urban area's transportation system make the area more attractive to employers and employees, and will presumably have the effect of increasing the urban area's population and employment. The analysis in chapter 3 and other evidence show that the effect is likely to be a slight upward shift accompanied by a flattening of the population density function. This means that the number of people living near the CBD will increase, but the percentage will fall. The effect of an increase in the urban area's population and employment on employment density functions is ambiguous, but the evidence in chapter 3 indicated that the density function would flatten in at least the manufacturing sector. The conclusion is that, to the extent that transportation improvements attract population and employment to the urban area, the effect on CBD employment and nearby population will be small. It is not possible to say whether the effect of transportation improvements on an urban area's population and employment will be large or small. It obviously depends on whether the improvement is made by just one or by a large groups of urban areas. Since no urban area has a monopoly of transportation technology, the relevant question would seem to be the effect of transportation improvements in a large group of metropolitan areas on the population and employment of the areas. Asked that way, the question is whether transportation improvements can change the size distribution of urban areas. Persistence of that size distribution across time and space is one of the best-documented social phenomena. It is extremely unlikely that the size distribution will be measurably affected by transportation improvements in a subset of metropolitan areas, unless the improvements are of the most dramatic kind.

The conclusion of these speculations is that urban transportation improvements may increase CBD employment slightly, but that the overall effect will be to flatten the urban area's population density function.

9

Suggestions for Further Research

In chapter 4, it was claimed that urban model building is an underdeveloped specialty in economics. I believe that the analysis in the last four chapters substantiates that claim. Although I hope that the models presented in those chapters have improved our understanding of the determinants of urban structure, it is clear that these and other published urban models are quite primitive. The purpose of this chapter is to discuss a variety of ways in which existing models could be extended and otherwise improved.

Of course, the way one extends or alters existing models depends in part on the goal one has in mind. An important goal, which seems dominant in the minds of many urban economists, is to extend the models so as to provide insight into public policy problems. The models in this monograph have had only peripheral relevance to public policy, and have not even contained a public sector. Nevertheless, some public policies could be analyzed with relatively minor modifications of these models. A few possibilities are sketched in the next section.

A second goal in extending and altering existing models is improvement in scientific understanding of the way urban economies work. Although the normative and positive goals are of course related, they do not usually lead to exactly the same research strategies. Economists' intuition suggests certain considerations that are the crucial ones to introduce into a model from the point of view of scientific understanding. These considerations may or may not facilitate policy evaluation. Aside from other considerations, limitations on research manpower and the capacity of computers may require that choices be made between models that will provide policy insight and those that will provide scientific understanding. Several extensions of existing models that are intended to improve scientific understanding are discussed in section 2.

1. Policy Evaluations

The easiest set of policies to study is that related to real estate taxes, and their effects can be studied within the model as it was developed in chapter 6. A uniform real estate tax on both land and improvements is simply a sales tax on housing services. Its analysis requires only the multiplication of $p_2(u)$ by a factor equal to one plus the tax rate. The price of housing services including the tax would appear in the demand function, equations (4) and (7) of chapter 6, but the price excluding the tax would appear in the factor demand equations (2) and (3) of chapter 6. Real estate taxes are paid by purchasers of housing services, but they are not received by owners of factors of production used to produce housing services. It would also be easy to analyze the effects of a differential real estate tax between central city and suburb. One might assume that the tax rate is one value, T_1, for all $u \leq u_1$, and another value, T_2, for all $u > u_1$. Of course, u_1 would have to be chosen so that $\epsilon < u_1 < u_A$, and presumably T_1 and T_2 would be chosen so that $T_1 > T_2$.

Urban renewal policy is a second public policy that would be interesting to analyze with models of urban structure, but an appropriate model would differ substantially from those presented in this monograph. One kind of urban renewal has to do with public policies to increase CBD output and employment. Effects of increases in N were analyzed in chapter 7. But the interesting questions can only be asked of a model in which employment can also be located outside the CBD. For that purpose, modifications of the model of the kind discussed in the next section are needed. Another kind of urban renewal has to do with public policies to improve housing in old and high density sections of the urban area. To analyze this kind of urban renewal, a minimum modification of the model would be to introduce capital depreciation into the production function for housing. Then analysis of renewal might go as follows: Solve the model to find the urban structure appropriate to the parameters at some time, t_1. Then suppose some parameters change so that the urban area grows to a larger size at some time, t_2. Suppose that the private market demolished the housing that existed at t_1 only if the capitalized increase in land rents that results when new housing is built exceeds the cost of demolishing the old housing. It is a condition for profitability of private renewal. The extent to which private renewal takes place will depend on depreciation rates and on demolition costs, as well as on the magnitude of the difference between existing and equilibrium land use. On this assumption, the model could be solved to see how growth would affect urban structure given that old housing is demolished only to the extent that is profitable. Then one could calculate, with the modified model, what the effect on urban structure would be if public renewal speeded up the demolition process. With a careful formulation of welfare criteria, one could also calculate whether public demolition and renewal would be desirable.

Perhaps the most interesting public policies to study would be those related to the transportation system. Each transportation mode has a production function (mostly permitting some input substitution within modes), a set of feasible pricing procedures, and ways of handling congestion. Each mode will therefore have a set of effects on urban structure. Also, each mode has an associated demand for its services that depends on price, congestion, and other conditions of service. It would be extremely interesting to compare the effects of alternative urban transportation systems on urban structure, using realistic production and demand functions. Much more difficult would be an evaluation of the welfare effects of alternative systems. The welfare effects would have to depend on the price, conditions of service, and congestion of the transportation system, and on the effect of the transportation system on the consumption of housing services.

Finally, some effects of zoning could be analyzed with no more than minor alterations of the model. Zoning requirements are of various kinds, but most either exclude certain kinds of employment or require that land input per residence exceeds a stipulated minimum. Employment restrictions can be analyzed only within a richer model of the kind discussed in section 2. But lot-size requirements can be analyzed with only minor modifications of the models presented here. Lot-size zoning often seems to work as follows: At some point in time a suburb is inhabited by people whose incomes and tastes indicate a certain optimum capital-land ratio in housing production. The residents control the political process in the suburb, and zoning regulations are promulgated that forbid smaller lots than are optimum for present residents. As time passes, the metropolitan area grows, land values rise, and the optimum capital-land ratio increases in the suburb. But the market is prevented from adjusting to the new equilibrium capital-land ratio by the zoning regulation. The purpose of the zoning regulation seems to be to keep out of the suburb people felt to be undesirable by the residents that control the political process. Clearly, the excluded people lose by the regulations. Existing residents gain in that they avoid neighbors they regard as undesirable, but it is not clear whether they gain or lose in terms of property values. Whether the foregoing is an accurate description of large-lot zoning or not, its effect is to impose specific residential densities on the land in parts of the urban area. That restriction could easily be introduced in the complex model and, with a specific welfare criterion, the welfare loss could be computed.

2. OTHER EXTENSIONS OF THE MODEL

From the point of view of scientific progress in urban model building, it seems clear that the urgent need is for models in which the amount and location of employment are endogenous. The model ought to be able to tell us how much employment the urban area can generate and where it will be located. Ideally, it ought to tell us that at least some employment will locate in various parts of the city, but the amounts ought to depend on the parameters of the model. Such a model could of course be used to study the causes and consequences of employment suburbanization.

I have spent considerable time and effort on such models, but have obtained almost no results. The following comments are made in the hope that they will be helpful to other urban model builders, at least in enabling them to avoid my mistakes.

One of the simplest models with endogenous employment might be as follows: Suppose that the production and consumption of housing services are as represented in chapter 6. Suppose also that, in addition to housing services, a single commodity is produced in the urban area. It is produced with a production function similar to equation (1) of chapter 6, but in which labor also appears as an input. There is a local demand for the commodity, similar to equation (4) of chapter 6. Both the price of the commodity and the price of housing services appear in the local demand equation for the commodity and in the demand equation for housing services.

There is also a nonlocal demand for the commodity, which depends on its price. The simplest assumption is that all units of the commodity to be exported outside the urban area must first be shipped to the center of the urban area, where there is a harbor, railhead, or expressway interchange. All exported units of the commodity must be sold at the same price at the city center, and the price at place of production must be less than the price at the city center by the cost of shipment from place of production to city center.

A more realistic assumption than the one in the previous paragraph would be that it is also possible to export the commodity, presumably by road, directly from its place of production and without shipping it to the city center. But a word of caution is needed here. The need to ship exports to the city center provides a reason for commodity production to take place in the urban area. If exports can be shipped outside the urban area directly from place of production, then there must be another force that keeps commodity production in the urban area or there will be no urban area.

Transportation services are produced with a production function, as in chapter 6. But the transportation system now must be used both by commuters and by shippers of the commodity. Both commuters and freight contribute to congestion. There are transportation cost functions, similar to equation (10) of chapter 6, for commuters and freight. At any u, transportation demand by commuters equals the excess of workers employed over workers resident between that u and the city center. The freight shipped through any value of u equals total production at larger values of u. Equations (11) through (13) of chapter 6 continue to hold with appropriate modifications. Specifically, it can be assumed that workers come to the urban area if they can earn an exogenously determined and competitive wage rate. The urban area's labor force therefore equals the number of workers demanded in commodity production at the predetermined wage rate.

The model described in the preceding paragraphs is much more cumbersome than the one presented in chapter 6. But some tedious manipulations make it possible to derive two differential equations, similar to equation (20) of chapter 6, for the rent offers of the housing and commodity production sectors. These two equations are simultaneous in that integrals analogous to that in equation (20) of chapter 6 contain rent offers of both sectors.

At any u, a sector would obtain the amount of land for which it can outbid the other sector. A large amount of frustrating computer work has led me to the following conclusions, which I cannot prove. First, all reasonable sets of parameter values allocate all available land close to the city center to commodity production and all land farther away from the center to housing services. Second, no reasonable set of parameter values exists such that some commodity production and some housing appear at the same u.

These conclusions are disappointing in that they imply that all commodity production takes place near the city center, as was assumed in chapter 6 and in my earlier model [19]. In other words, they preclude the possibility of suburbanization of commodity production, regardless of which, among reasonable sets of parameter values, is chosen. An uninteresting exception occurs if production functions are identical for the production of commodities and housing services. But that means that the model cannot tell the difference between commuters and freight!

It is not clear why the model described in this section cannot locate both housing and commodity production at the same u. Something in the model implies that if it is worthwhile to use a little of the land available at a certain u for some activity, then it is worthwhile to use all the land available at that u for the same activity. It may be that the Cobb-Douglas production function has too few degrees of freedom to permit a richer result. Or, it may be that constant returns to scale preclude a richer result. Of course, the model assumes constant returns only in commodity and housing service production, and not in congestion and transportation cost.

The tentative results stated above for the model outlined in this section are similar to results established in chapter 5 for the simple model with fixed production coefficients. In that model, it was also found that markets either completely segregated commodity production and housing (so that there was no suburbanization of production) or that they completely integrated commodity production and housing (so that there was no commuting). It is surprising and disappointing that this dichotomous result carries to the more complex model outlined above.

It is an open question whether a different model that retained constant returns in production could produce partial suburbanization of employment. It would be valuable to answer the question because spatial models with increasing returns are extremely difficult to specify in a satisfactory way. In any case, the profession awaits the first mathematical model that will provide significant insight into the causes and mechanisms of employment suburbanization.

It seems clear that the assumption of constant returns must be dropped if models are to be produced that include another phenomenon prominent in modern urban areas, namely subcenters. For the purpose of this discussion, a subcenter is an area, away from the city center, where land rents are higher than they are somewhat closer to the center. On this definition, subcenters entail land-rent functions that are not monotonic. Subcenters are, of course, common in the suburbs of large urban areas. Suburban shopping centers are examples. But more interesting are the clusters of commercial and manufacturing activity, often taking place in buildings considerably higher than those closer to the city center, that appear in the suburbs of many central cities. Evidently, such clusters are subject to scale and other economies similar to those that produce agglomeration in the CBD. But these activities exhaust their economies at a scale that does not require central location. So much is fairly clear and was discussed briefly in chapter 1. But inclusion of this phenomenon in formal models awaits further research.

REFERENCES AND BIBLIOGRAPHY

[1] Alonso, William. *Location and Land Use*. Cambridge: Harvard University Press, 1964.

[2] Arrow, Kenneth J. "Applications of Control Theory to Economic Growth." *Lectures in Applied Mathematics*, vol. 12 (Mathematics of the Decision Sciences, Part 2), 1968, pp. 85–119.

[3] Bartholomew, Harland. *Land Uses in American Cities*. Cambridge: Harvard University Press, 1955.

Beckmann, Martin, see Koopmans.

Bogue, Donald, see Kitagawa.

[4] Chapin, F. Stuart, and Weiss, Shirley. "A Probabilistic Model for Urban Growth." *Transportation Research*, 2 (1968): 375–90.

[5] Clark, Colin. "Urban Population Densities." *Journal of the Royal Statistical Society*, Series A, 114 (1951): 490–96.

[6] Crecine, John. *A Dynamic Model of Urban Structure*. Rand Corporation, P–3803, March 1968.

Dee, Norbert, see Mills.

[7] Duncan, Otis Dudley, and others. *Metropolis and Region*. Baltimore: The Johns Hopkins Press, 1960.

[8] Forrester, Jay W. *Industrial Dynamics*. New York: Massachusetts Institute of Technology Press and John Wiley and Sons, Inc., 1961.

[9] ———. *Urban Dynamics*. Cambridge: Massachusetts Institute of Technology Press, 1969.

[10] Friedlaender, Ann. *The Dilemma of Freight Transport Regulation*. Washington: Brookings Institution, 1969.

[11] Harris, Britton. *Quantitative Models of Urban Development: Their Role in Metropolitan Policy-Making*. Institute of Environmental Studies, University of Pennsylvania, 1967.

Harwitz, Mitchell, see Mohring.

Hearle, Edward, see Niedercorn.

143

[12] Hoch, Irving. "The Three-Dimensional City: Contained Urban Space." In *The Quality of the Urban Environment*, edited by Harvey Perloff, pp. 75–138. Washington: Resources for the Future, 1969.
Kain, John, see Meyer; Niedercorn.

[13] Kitagawa, Evelyn, and Bogue, Donald. *Suburbanization of Manufacturing Activity Within Standard Metropolitan Areas.* Oxford, Ohio: Scripps Foundation, 1955.

[14] Koopmans, Tjalling C., and Beckmann, Martin. "Assignment Problems and the Location of Economic Activities." *Econometrica*, 25 (1957): 53–76.

[15] Lösch, August. *The Economics of Location.* New Haven: Yale University Press, 1954.

[16] Lowry, Ira S. *A Model of Metropolis.* Rand Corporation, RM–4035–RC, August 1964.

[17] ———. *Seven Models of Urban Development: A Structural Comparison.* Rand Corporation, P–3673, September 1967.

[18] Meyer, John; Kain, John; and Wohl, Martin. *The Urban Transportation Problem.* Cambridge: Harvard University Press, 1965.

[19] Mills, Edwin S. "An Aggregative Model of Resource Allocation in a Metropolitan Area." *American Economic Review*, 57 (1967): 197–210.

[20] ———. "The Value of Urban Land." In *The Quality of the Urban Environment*, edited by Harvey Perloff, pp. 231–53. Baltimore: The Johns Hopkins Press, 1969.

[21] ———. "The Efficiency of Spatial Competition." *Papers and Proceedings of the Regional Science Association*, 25 (1970): 71–82.

[22] ———. "Urban Density Functions." *Urban Studies*, 7 (1970): 5–20.

[23] ———, and Dee, Norbert. "Numerical Analysis of a General Equilibrium Model of a Metropolitan Area," unpublished manuscript.

[24] Mohring, Herbert, and Harwitz, Mitchell. *Highway Benefits: An Analytical Approach.* Evanston, Ill.: Northwestern University Press, 1962.

[25] Moses, Leon, and Williamson, Harold. "Location of Economic Activity in Cities." *American Economic Review*, 57 (1967): 211–22.

[26] Muth, Richard. *Cities and Housing.* Chicago: University of Chicago Press, 1969.

[27] Niedercorn, John. *An Econometric Model of Metropolitan Employment and Population Growth.* Rand Corporation, RM–3758–RC, October 1963.

[28] ———, and Hearle, Edward. *Recent Land-Use Trends in Forty-Eight Large American Cities.* Rand Corporation, RM–3664–1–FF, September 1963.

[29] ———, and Kain, John. *Suburbanization of Employment and Population 1948–1975.* Rand Corporation, P–2641, January 1963.

[30] Perloff, Harvey, and others. *Regions, Resources, and Economic Growth.* Baltimore: The Johns Hopkins Press, 1960.

[31] Reid, Margaret. *Housing and Income.* Chicago: University of Chicago Press, 1962.

[32] Scarborough, James. *Numerical Mathematical Analysis.* 6th ed. Baltimore: The Johns Hopkins Press, 1966. Newton-Raphson

[33] Vickery, William. "Pricing as a Tool in Coordination of Local Transportation." In *Transportation Economics*, edited by John Meyer. New York: National Bureau of Economic Research, 1965.

[34] Walters, Alan. "Theory and Measurement of Private and Social Cost of Highway Congestion." *Econometrica*, 29 (1961): 676–99.

[35] Weber, Alfred. *Theory of the Location of Industries*. Chicago: University of Chicago Press, 1928.

Weiss, Shirley, see Chapin.

Williamson, Harold, see Moses.

[36] Wingo, Lowdon. *Transportation and Urban Land*. Washington: Resources for the Future, 1961.

Wohl, Martin, see Meyer.

Index

Agglomeration, determinants of, 5–9
Alonso, William, 64, 67–71, 73, 75, 96
Amenity resources. *See* Resources
Annexation, 24–25, 34
Arrow, Kenneth J., 86n

Bartholomew, Harland, 47
Beckmann, Martin, 89
Bertrand, Trent, 81n
Bogue, Donald, 36
Bradford, David, 81n
Business, in Forrester's model, 78–79

Call-a-Computer Corporation, 107n
Capital, rental rate on, 99, 100, 124, 126–27
Capital-land ratio, 93–101 *passim*, 131, 139
Census, 23, 25; data limitations, 34–35
Census Bureau, U.S., 35
Central business district (CBD), 112; commuting distance to, 37, 97, 98; costs of commuting to, 96–104 *passim*, 113, 115, 116; employment in, 76, 96–97, 103, 111, 135, 136, 138; production in, 126; transportation to, 134, 135, 136
Central city: boundaries of, 24–25, 34; density and commuting distance from CBD, 37; growth rates of, 28t; population and employment in, 26, 27t, 28t

Central city–suburb dichotomy, 24, 34, 35
Chapin, F. Stuart, 73–75
Chicago metropolitan area, 38
Cities: assumptions accounting for, 5–9; definition of, 3; distress alleviation programs in, 79; function of, 9
City center, distance from, 50, 64, 67, 68, 76–77, 83, 97–104 *passim*, 116, 117, 118
Clark, Colin, 36, 37, 56, 77, 123
Commodities. *See* Goods
Commuting: between SMSAs, 14; costs of, 5, 51, 64, 65, 68, 84–94 *passim*, 96–117 *passim*, 118–27 *passim*, 135; distance, 37, 50, 64, 68, 76, 85, 87–88, 97–104 *passim*, 116, 117, 118; housing location and commuting cost relationship, 96–127; outward, 85, 89; and production facility location, 85–86
Computer, aid in solving model, 104–8
Congestion, 8, 112, 139; costs of, 113, 116, 123, 124, 125, 133, 134–35; model with, 96–108
Construction, 78, 79
Crecine, John, 73

Dee, Norbert, 126
Density functions (*see also under* Employment; Manufacturing; Population): determinants of, 50–57; estimating, 35–36, 38–40, 44; flattening, 37, 43, 44, 46, 56, 57, 63, 96, 97, 136; linear

Note: n = footnote, *t* = table, *f* = figure.

147